Using
EQUITY
AUDITS

Create

Equi DATE DUE nt

Using
EQUITY
AUDITS
to Create
Equitable and Excellent
Schools

LINDA SKRLA
KATHRYN BELL McKENZIE
JAMES JOSEPH SCHEURICH

Foreword by Judith Richardson, Director
Diversity, Equity, and Urban Initiatives, NASSP

A JOINT PUBLICATION

nsdc

CORWIN
A SAGE Company

NATIONAL ASSOCIATION
OF SECONDARY SCHOOL
PRINCIPALS

For information:

Corwin
A SAGE Company
2455 Teller Road
Thousand Oaks, California 91320
(800) 233-9936
Fax: (800) 417-2466
www.corwinpress.com

SAGE India Pvt. Ltd.
B 1/I 1 Mohan Cooperative Industrial Area
Mathura Road, New Delhi 110 044
India

SAGE Ltd.
1 Oliver's Yard
55 City Road
London EC1Y 1SP
United Kingdom

SAGE Asia-Pacific Pte. Ltd.
33 Pekin Street #02-01
Far East Square
Singapore 048763

Printed in the United States of America

Library of Congress Cataloging-in-Publication Data

Skrla, Linda, 1957–
Using equity audits to create equitable and excellent schools / Linda Skrla, Kathryn Bell McKenzie, James Joseph Scheurich.
        p. cm.
"A Joint Publication With the National Association of Secondary School Principals and the National Staff Development Council."
Includes bibliographical references and index.
ISBN 978-1-4129-3932-4 (pbk.)
    1. School improvement programs—United States. 2. Educational equalization—United States—Evaluation. I. McKenzie, Kathryn Bell. II. Scheurich, James Joseph, 1944–
III. National Association of Secondary School Principals (U.S.) IV. National Staff Development Council (U.S.) V. Title.

LB2822.82.S49 2009
379.2′60973—dc22   2009002802

This book is printed on acid-free paper.

09   10   11   12   13   10   9   8   7   6   5   4   3   2   1

Acquisitions Editor:	Arnis Burvikovs
Associate Editor:	Desirée A. Bartlett
Production Editor:	Jane Haenel
Copy Editor:	Jeannette McCoy
Typesetter:	C&M Digitals (P), Ltd.
Proofreader:	Marleis Roberts
Indexer:	Sylvia Coates
Cover and Graphic Designer:	Michael Dubowe

Contents

Foreword

In this country and at this time, it is fitting that we should talk about leading diverse communities. Demographers now predict that "minorities" will constitute the majority of schoolchildren by 2023, a projection that challenges leaders to provide educational opportunities in a nurturing environment that will enable *every* student to achieve academically.

Using Equity Audits to Create Equitable and Excellent Schools takes a focused, logical look at the culture that exists in our schools and, through data coaching and self-evaluation, encourages school leaders to identify factors that may be fueling the lingering achievement gap. This book addresses the realization that we might have structures in place that inhibit academic success for every student in our schools.

A 2005 report by The Education Trust labeled "disappointing" the progress we have made on closing the achievement gaps among income, gender, and ethnic subgroups. "A primary goal of NCLB was to close persistent gaps in achievement. Many states are not achieving that goal in secondary schools." The report goes on to state, "In reading and math, for instance, both the Latino-White gap and the gap between poor and non-poor students grew or stayed the same in more states than they narrowed" (The Education Trust, 2005, p. 2).

Closing the gap means overcoming many complex issues, such as low expectations for students, underdeveloped language skills, and lack of equity in teacher quality, program participation, and resources. Research has shown that learning for diverse and low-income students is school based. Given this knowledge, instructional leaders must address the disparity in achievement through school initiatives that specifically address the culture surrounding rigor in secondary schools.

Principals and leadership teams grapple with the charge of ensuring that every student will meet increased academic standards, and district and school system officials are challenged with making every school a high performing one. This book finally provides a focused and logical way to improve student achievement by implementing effective school culture change.

Using Equity Audits to Create Equitable and Excellent Schools has many assets. For educators whose time is at a premium, an overview of the research appears at the beginning of the book, with the practical applications following. Each chapter is structured with both succinct summaries and a full explanation for those who need only to understand the vision and those who need enough in-depth information to realize it. This book discusses who should be chosen for the leadership team as well as addresses other crucial questions: Who will be the change agents in your school? Who are the effective analysts of your school culture and the catalysts for a culture change? How do you raise the equity consciousness among teachers? How do you raise the expectation level for each student they touch? There are practical examples throughout the book based on local school data, with pointers about having critical conversations with all staff and stakeholders. In addition, case studies help school implementation teams avoid potential traps.

The equity self-assessment process is focused in three major areas for schools and school systems: teacher quality equity, program equity, and achievement equity. Assessment in these three areas uses local school data or district group data to help establish where a school or a school district currently is in providing academic equity for each student. Additionally, one chapter details the concept of data coaching for quality instruction and provides practical implementation examples. Finally, the administrator and leadership team are provided with tools for documenting where the school stands and where it needs to go to become culturally equitable for each student.

It is serendipitous how closely this audit process follows the recommended framework of the *Breaking Ranks* school improvement series and complements *Breaking Ranks: A Field Guide for Leading Change.* As Gerald Tirozzi, executive director of the National Association of Secondary School Principals, charges in the *Breaking Ranks* improvement series, changing a culture requires more than being the first person with a great idea. *Transformations do not take place until the culture of the school permits it, and no long-term, significant change can take place without creating a culture to sustain that change.* Leaders at all levels must foster this transformed environment.

The question for educational leaders is, How can we foster these cultural changes within schools so that we can lead improvement? Seize the opportunity to demonstrate to others what most of us in education already know—that great school leaders have the will, expertise, and determination to create a culture that challenges and educates each student. Properly implemented, the *Breaking Ranks* framework can reach every student. Properly sustained, whole school improvement leads to high-quality education for all.

Judith Richardson
Director of Equity, Diversity,
and Urban Initiatives
National Association of
Secondary School Principals

REFERENCE

The Education Trust. (2005, January). *Stalled in secondary: A look at student achievement since the No Child Left Behind Act.* Retrieved at http://www2 .edtrust.org/NR/rdonlyres/77670E50-188F-4AA8-8729-555115389E18/ 0/StalledInSecondary.pdf

Acknowledgments

The authors wish first to thank the educators and leaders on the campuses and in the school districts that have worked with us in our research over the past fifteen years. We have learned much about leadership for equity and excellence because these schools and districts opened their doors and allowed us access to their day-to-day practice. The insights gained through this field research shape the discussion that appears in this book. Thanks especially to Antoinette Riester-Wood, Alicia Thomas, and Judith Moening from North East Independent School District in San Antonio, Texas, for sharing their story of the development of the Data Coaching model that appears in Chapter 7.

In addition, we wish to thank the foundations that have generously sponsored our research—the Sid W. Richardson Foundation (Valleau Wilke, Jr., Executive Vice President), the William and Flora Hewlett Foundation (Marshall Smith, Education Program Director), and the Houston Endowment (George Grainger, Senior Grant Officer). Without the vision of these individuals and the significant investment of these foundations in research on educational success in schools and districts serving primarily children of color and children from low-income homes, this book would not have been possible.

Also, sincere thanks to the graduate students in our classes at Texas A&M University; our interactions with these professionals who are out on the front lines in schools in the highly diverse state of Texas have been invaluable as we consistently strive to keep the bridge passable between research and practice. This equity and excellence leadership tool, equity audits, finally has become a stand-alone book, in fact, mainly because our students have found our earlier, article-length, treatment of the topic useful in their schools and districts and have asked for more material and strategies to use in their practice.

We wish also to thank the nine reviewers solicited by Corwin to comment on this work. Their critique and suggestions for improvement have been extremely helpful to us in making this a better book.

LINDA'S ACKNOWLEDGMENTS

Thanks and great affection go first to the owners of the other two thirds of the "collective brain" that produces this research on equity audits and other closely related topics—my coauthors, Kathryn and Jim. I'm blessed as a scholar and as a person to have colleagues and friends such as these. Two other people who are both scholarly colleagues and dear friends that I wish to thank for their support are Andrea Rorrer and Michelle Young; I would never have made it in academe without them. A big thank you also to graduate assistants extraordinaire Kimberly Dickerson (now an Assistant Professor at Southern University) and Noelle Eason.

In addition, love and thanks to my mom and my sister Sandie for believing in me always. Much love and appreciation also to my three amazing sons—Steve, Scott, and Eric—for their encouragement, support, and unwavering belief that their mom rocks. And, on a related note, thanks to the members of the rock band Journey, past and present, for their incredible music that has helped keep my head alive for over thirty years. To the friends I have made through their fan club, especially Debbie, Tom, Gayle, Jen, Dan, and Sky, you guys rock, too!

KATHRYN'S ACKNOWLEDGMENTS

First, I acknowledge my coauthors, Linda and Jim, who are not only incredible colleagues but also are my friends—critical, spiritual, dear friends. They are as much a part of me as I am a part of all things. Second, I acknowledge my children, Kelsey and Kolter, who are amazing adults. They are my constant reminder that every child is someone's child—a blessing and an opportunity to realize the world as we want it to be. Third, to Nils and Macy, my canine companions, who sit with me on the porch under the big sky and trees in Texas while I write and remind me that I'm important but not that important. Last, to Martyn, who sometimes leads and sometimes follows and sometimes just holds on, but who always loves me.

JIM'S ACKNOWLEDGMENTS

My homage, praise, and thanks go to Linda and Kathryn for being the primary authors of this book and for allowing me to be a small part of this project.

PUBLISHER'S ACKNOWLEDGMENTS

Corwin gratefully acknowledges the contributions of the following individuals:

Tonya Gau Bartell, Assistant Professor
University of Delaware, School of Education
Newark, DE

Nic Cooper, Director of Secondary Student Services
Union School
Saline, MI

Cheryl Gray, Leadership Curriculum Development and Training Coordinator
Southern Regional Education Board
Atlanta, GA

Janet Hurt, Associate Superintendent
Logan County Schools
Russellville, KY

Mary Johnstone, Principal
Rabbit Creek Elementary School
Anchorage, AK

Lawrence Kohn, Associate Professor
Sam Houston State University
Huntsville, TX

Amanda Mayeaux, Associate Principal
Donaldsonville High School
Donaldsonville, LA

Judith A. Rogers, Professional Learning Specialist
Tucson Unified School District
Tucson, AZ

Sara E. Spruce, Professor of Education
Olivet Nazarene University
Bourbonnais, IL

About the Authors

 **Linda Skrla** is a professor of educational administration and the associate dean for research and P-16 initiatives in the College of Education and Human Development at Texas A&M University. She holds a PhD from the University of Texas at Austin and has extensive experience as a public school teacher and administrator. Her research focuses on equity issues in school leadership and policy, including accountability, highly successful school districts, and women super-intendents. Her work has appeared in numerous journals, and she has coauthored or coedited four other books, including *Leadership for Equity and Excellence: Creating High-Achievement Classrooms, Schools, and Districts* (Corwin, 2003) and *Accountability and Equity: Policies, Paradigms, and Politics* (RoutledgeFalmer, 2003).

 **Kathryn Bell McKenzie** is an associate professor in the Department of Educational Administration and Human Resource Development at Texas A&M University in College Station. Her research foci include equity and social justice in schools, school leadership, qualitative methodology, and critical white studies. During her over twenty years in public education, she was a classroom teacher, curriculum specialist, assistant principal, and principal.

 **James Joseph Scheurich** is a professor and the head of the Department of Educational Administration and Human Resource Development at Texas A&M University. His research interests include equity in education, schools and districts that are successful with diverse students, race and racism, educational accountability, and qualitative research methodologies.

He is the editor of a research journal, serves on the editorial boards of several research journals, has written over thirty-five articles for research journals, and has published five books. He has served on several committees for national research organizations and is currently on the Executive Committee for the University Council for Educational Administration (UCEA). In 2006, he received the UCEA Master Professor Award for helping prepare so many successful young professors in his research field, and he was a 2008 nominee for president of the American Educational Research Association (AERA).

Part I

Background and Context for Equity Audits

1 Introduction

Ethics and equity and the principles of justice do not change with the calendar.

—D. H. Lawrence

There is currently a large national focus on closing school achievement gaps, but practical information for school leaders to actually use in their efforts to close these gaps is in short supply. That is the purpose of this book—to provide such practical information in the form of an expanded discussion of equity audits, a school leadership tool presented previously as a single chapter in *Leadership for Equity and Excellence: Creating High-Achievement Classrooms, Schools, and Districts*, our 2003 Corwin book.

Equity audits are a systematic way for school leaders—principals, superintendents, curriculum directors, teacher leaders—to assess the degree of equity or inequity present in three key areas of their schools or districts: programs, teacher quality, and achievement. These equity audits are designed to put streamlined, practical strategies in the hands of leadership practitioners at a time when such tools are sorely needed.

In keeping with our goal of providing a useful book, we think readers will find it useful if we make clear right at the beginning of this book what we mean by the word *equity*. Understanding how we use the term is central to understanding our discussion of equity audits in the rest of the book. By equity, we mean explicitly *educational equity*, an excellent definition of which is found on the Wisconsin Department of Public Instruction's Web site:

Education equity: the educational policies, practices and programs necessary to (a) eliminate educational barriers based on gender, race/ethnicity, national origin, color, disability, age, or other protected group status; and (b) provide equal educational opportunities and ensure that historically underserved or underrepresented populations meet the same rigorous standards for academic performance expected of all children and youth. Educational equity knowledge and practices in public schools have evolved over time and require a comprehensive approach. Equity strategies are planned, systemic, and focus on the core of the teaching and learning process (curriculum, instruction, and school environment/culture). Educational equity activities promote the real possibility of equality of educational results for each student and between diverse groups of students.

This definition of education equity highlights the complexity of the conditions required to achieve it and also emphasizes that its realization is dependent on addressing inequities in access, programs, and results—themes that we highlight consistently in the chapters ahead.

We also wish to emphasize here that our discussion of educational equity in general and equity audits specifically is intended primarily for educational leaders at the campus and district levels. That is because educational leaders are on the front lines in the ongoing battle to achieve education equity in U.S. public schools.

Though substantial educational achievement gaps have existed throughout the history of U.S. schooling, the national focus on closing them has never been more intense. The No Child Left Behind Act of 2001 (NCLB) was signed into law on January 8, 2002, and could be described as the most sweeping reform of U.S. federal education policy since the 1960s. Although changes and modifications have been made to the law, and others likely will continue in the future, at its center remains a *potentially* revolutionary idea—an explicit statement by the federal government that achievement gaps between white and middle- and upper-income children, on one hand, and children of color and children from low-income homes, on the other, are unacceptable and must be eliminated.

This is an important policy statement from the national government; however, its success in achieving the aim of closing achievement gaps ultimately will depend on the law's implementation by hundreds of thousands of educators around the country. This is where school leaders play an extremely important role. They act as policy mediators or street-level bureaucrats (Lipsky, 1980; Rorrer & Skrla, 2005), in filtering and shaping the ways policies (such as NCLB) are implemented in local schools. In other words, school leaders such as principals can block the policies, ignore them, use them in negative ways, or use them in positive ways. We want to maximize leaders' ability to use accountability policy (including NCLB) that is intended to eliminate achievement gaps in the most positive and productive ways possible.

For such positive use of accountability policy to actually happen, however, school leaders need to be assisted in understanding how the force of these polices can be applied to help them achieve the goals they have for their schools, including reducing and eventually eliminating achievement gaps. One of the prime ways accountability at the national, state, and local levels can be of concrete assistance to school leaders is utilizing the data these systems provide to assess the current state of the school or district and to track progress.

Although many state accountability systems, and increasingly the federal system, have been producing this type of data for the past fifteen or twenty years, the simple existence of the data does not automatically lead to school improvement or to diminished achievement gaps. The data must be analyzed, and school decision making must be linked to the data. This sounds like a straightforward process, but it is considerably more complicated in actual practice, particularly when the data show wide gaps in achievement between and among student groups based on race, ethnicity, family income, and language proficiency.

We have found in our work over the past two decades as researchers and as teachers who work with aspiring and practicing school administrators that people in schools overwhelmingly do not have a clear, accurate, or useful understanding of the degree of inequity present in their own schools and school districts. Furthermore, in typical school settings, teachers and administrators frequently avoid the topic of race completely as a possible factor in discussions about achievement gaps (Pollock, 2001). In addition, it is also common that when questioned about why children of color and children from low-income homes do not do well in school, educators almost always give reasons external to schools as the cause, such as the children's parents, their neighborhoods, and even their genetics (Haycock, 2001).

Thus, educators, school leaders in particular, need assistance in learning to recognize that there are large and persistent patterns of inequity *internal* to schools—patterns that are embedded in the many assumptions, beliefs, practices, procedures, and policies of schools themselves. In fact, as one of our reviewers pointed out, such patterns of inequity not only result in differential experiences for students who differ along race, social class, gender, and disability lines, the systemic inequity present in schools may actually create differences among students (see also McDermott, 1997). Therefore, in response to this need for assistance in identifying and addressing internal patterns of inequity, equity audits are intended to provide such assistance in a very concrete way. In other words, these audits are designed to provide insight into, discussion of, and practical responses to systemic patterns of inequity in schools and school districts. Our discussion of equity audits continues in more depth and detail in the next eleven chapters.

CHAPTERS 2–12 PREVIEWS

The chapters in this book are roughly divided into three parts. The first part of the book (Chapters 1–3) contains more theoretical content; these chapters lay out the background and historical context for our version of equity audits. Part II (Chapters 4–7) describes the equity audit process for schools and districts. In Chapters 8 through 12 (Part III), we concentrate on attitudes, beliefs, strategies, and examples that are intended to help leaders address inequities uncovered by equity audits in their schools and districts. A brief preview of the content of each individual chapter follows.

Chapter 2. The Case for Systemic Equity

In this chapter, we include a discussion of historic inequities in U.S. public schools, offer a brief history of successive "waves" of school reform, and make the case for the need for systemic equity. That is, we argue that achievement equity is not possible without equity in other parts of the system, specifically teacher-quality equity and equity in the instructional programs to which children have access.

Chapter 3. History and Overview of Equity Audits

Here we trace the three streams of earlier research on which our version of equity audits builds—civil rights, curriculum management audits, and state accountability systems. We also suggest a simple process for conducting equity audits and provide the overall model that will be expanded upon in Chapters 4, 5, and 6.

Chapter 4. Teacher Quality Equity

This chapter explains and provides examples for the four indicators of teacher quality equity: (a) teacher education (bachelor's, master's, and doctoral degrees; number or percentage holding a particular degree), (b) teacher experience (number of years as a teacher), (c) teacher mobility (number or percentage of teachers leaving or not leaving a campus on an annual basis), and (d) teachers without certification or assigned outside of their area of teaching expertise (e.g., language arts teachers teaching a math course).

Chapter 5. Programmatic Equity

This chapter provides explanation and examples for the second component of the equity audit, programmatic equity, which includes four indicators that research has consistently shown to be significant sites of inequity. These four include the following: (a) special education, (b) gifted and talented education (G/T), (c) bilingual education, and (d) student discipline.

Chapter 6. Achievement Equity

Here we provide explanation and examples for the third audit area, achievement equity, including the four indicators: (a) state achievement test results, (b) dropout rates, (c) high school graduation tracks, and (d) SAT/ACT/AP/IB results.

Chapter 7. Equity Audits for School Districts

This chapter extends the equity audit model to the school district level and provides an extended illustration of how one district operationalized district-level equity auditing.

Chapter 8. Strategies: Becoming an Equity-Oriented Change Agent

This chapter focuses on leaders acquiring and maintaining the equity attitude required to implement equity audits. The leadership to implement the equity audit requires a change agent, and being a successful change agent requires skills and assumptions for working with others. Chapter 8 discusses these skills and assumptions, many of which we have learned from or have had reinforced by our own efforts to be change agents.

Chapter 9. Strategies: Increasing Equity Consciousness Among Teachers

In this chapter and Chapter 10, we discuss two aspects of improving teaching: equity consciousness and well-developed teaching skills. Chapter 9 focuses specifically on equity consciousness. First, we define the four central beliefs on which an equity consciousness is built. Next, we describe the four levels of a developing equity consciousness. Finally, we offer strategies instructional leaders can use to help themselves and teachers further develop their equity consciousness.

Chapter 10. Strategies: Developing High-Quality Teaching Skills

This chapter focuses on the second aspect of teacher quality: well-developed teaching skills. In this chapter, we offer nine teaching skills that high quality teachers employ. Included with each skill is an evidence statement to assist one in knowing what this skill would look like in practice. We conclude Chapter 10 with strategies for helping teachers develop high quality teaching skills.

Chapter 11. Strategies: Avoiding Equity Traps and Developing Equity Skills

In this chapter, we define and give examples of the traps that prevent schools from being successful with all students, what we call "equity traps." Additionally, we describe and offer examples of a matching set of "equity skills" that prevent one from falling into these traps or allow one to be released from these traps. In this chapter, we also provide strategies to assist leaders in helping themselves, and those who work alongside them in schools, to develop their equity skills.

Chapter 12. Conclusion

Here we provide a review and summary of the main concepts outlined in the book.

CHAPTER CONCLUSION

Our overall goal for this book is to describe and discuss equity audits with an emphasis on detail and practicality that was not possible in our earlier discussions of this topic due to space limitations. We see equity audits as an important tool for educational leaders' toolboxes—one that has the potential to be extremely useful in the current highly pressurized accountability climate in U.S. public education.

2 The Case for Systemic Equity

It occurs to me that systemic equity can only be created in an environment that embraces a set of underlying assumptions about the right of every learner to receive the best possible public education.

—Bradley Scott

Accountability policy at the state and national levels has been the largest issue in U.S. education for the past two decades. The issues associated with accountability, particularly standardized testing, have generated huge amounts of public, media, and educator attention. Though this focus on accountability began in some states in the mid 1980s (Smith & O'Day, 1990), the passage of the federal No Child Left Behind Act (NCLB) in 2001 and subsequent modifications of the law have increased both the pressure of accountability on schools and public awareness of it.

Thus, educational researchers and practitioners also have been increasingly focused on accountability policy and its effects over the past twenty years. There has been a great deal of debate over the effects of such policies on states, districts, schools, teachers, and students. A particularly heated area of these debates has been the equity effects of such policies. A central question has been whether accountability polices and standardized testing are helping or harming those children the policies are most often designed to serve. These include children from low-income homes, children of color, children who are English language learners, and children with learning differences.

ACCOUNTABILITY AND EDUCATIONAL EQUITY

Unfortunately, much of the debate in both practitioner and research circles on the relationship between accountability and equity has been carried out in overly simplistic, "all good" or "all bad" terms. This has resulted in a polarization, or choosing of sides, among many educators and educational researchers. People are assumed either to be "for" accountability or "against" it, leaving a large expanse of middle ground unexplored and uninhabited (Elmore, 2002).

The three authors of this book, former practitioners and now researchers, have spent much of the past fifteen years arguing for the value of exploring that middle ground. We have repeatedly pointed out in our earlier work (see McKenzie, 2003; Scheurich, Skrla, & Johnson, 2000; Skrla, 2001; Skrla, Scheurich, Johnson, & Koschoreck, 2001a; for a few examples) that the relationships between accountability and educational equity are definitely not as simple as many people want to make them out to be. These relationships are instead very complicated, dynamic (changing constantly), and messily interwoven with other things going on in schools. We have also repeatedly reminded people that there is a large amount of research showing a whole range of the effects of accountability from negative to neutral to positive.

The main point we want to emphasize here is this: If the ongoing conversation among practitioners and researchers about equity and accountability is actually going to help provide real equity for real children who have been at the destructive end of the achievement gap, we all have to get beyond this good versus bad conversation. The extreme complexity of accountability systems and their equally dynamic, complex effects requires that we all engage one another in respectful ways and learn to give careful consideration to viewpoints different from our own (O'Day, 2002).

In our attempts to live up to what we are asking others to do, over the past several years, we have participated in accountability debates and discussions in numerous practitioner and research venues, including journals, conferences, books, and inservice sessions for schools and school districts. In all of these places, we have repeated our call for a more complex understanding of the accountability policy systems, their effects, and their implementations.

We have also been very clear about our support for some aspects of accountability policy because of several positive equity effects we see, including (a) providing clear, common expectations for student achievement for all student groups; (b) focusing public attention on achievement gaps; (c) providing accountability data for use by parents, community groups, and the media; and (d) holding district and school leaders accountable for educating literally all students.

However, we want to say clearly here that we have also learned a great deal from those who disagree with us and those who criticize our work (see Anderson, 2001; Haney, 2001; Klein, 2001; Sclafani, 2001; Trueba, 2001; and Valencia, Valenzuela, Sloan, & Foley, 2001). Based on debates, dialogs, and discussions with people who are not as supportive of accountability policy as we have been, our viewpoints have evolved. We now have an increased and more nuanced appreciation for the fact that accountability policy alone is not enough to support the large improvement of educational practices that will be required in order to reduce and eventually eliminate achievement gaps in every school in every district across the United States.

A few examples of critics who helped change (and we would say improve) our understanding of the relationships between accountability policy and educational equity include Walt Haney (2001), who has been convincing in his arguments that reducing school dropout rates is as critically important as is increasing student academic achievement. Also, Richard Valencia and his colleagues (2001) constructively argue that teacher quality is an extremely important factor that has large effects on what children learn. Larry Parker (2001) is another colleague who has highlighted the importance of overrepresentation of children of color in special education and the differential educational progress of African American boys and girls as critical issues that also influence educational equity.

Our view, then, of the relationship between accountability and educational equity has matured, grown, and developed, as we hope it has for others. Our earlier work concentrated mainly on schools and districts demonstrating progress in closing achievement gaps, and we particularly focused on achievement equity. In our more recent work, we have begun to concentrate more on the systemic nature of both the gaps and the progress toward closing them. Much of the content of the "strategies" chapters that appear in the second half of this book resulted from this evolution in our research focus in response to dialog with our critics.

Thus, accountability policy, with its heavy reliance on standardized testing, remains to us a very powerful and important force in working toward educational equity. However, we see it clearly as only one of several parts in a larger system of both equitable and inequitable school practices. To reach the goal of reducing and eventually eliminating achievement gaps, we argue that a broader approach to educational equity, a *systemic equity*, be required.

SYSTEMIC EQUITY DEFINED

A useful definition of systemic equity was provided by Scott's (2001, March) writing for the Intercultural Development Research Association (IDRA):

> Systemic equity is defined as the transformed ways in which systems and individuals habitually operate to ensure that every learner—in whatever learning environment that learner is found—has the greatest opportunity to learn enhanced by the resources and supports necessary to achieve competence, excellence, independence, responsibility, and self-sufficiency for school and for life. (p. 6)

In other words, systemic equity requires that equity be present in all parts of the educational system, including environment and resources, rather than just to be focused narrowly on achievement equity.

A somewhat different, more expanded view of what systemic equity in education would look like was outlined in 1994 by the National Coalition of Equity Advocates in what they called the Principles of Equity in Education (Box 2.1).

BOX 2.1

Principles of Equity in Education

- Each student must be provided powerful curricula through adequate instructional and support systems to give him or her the opportunity to learn and the expectation to learn to the highest content and performance standards established for other students in his or her school, district, and state.
- Each family and community within a local education agency's jurisdiction must have access to the information, health and social services, and the participatory opportunity ties necessary to assure their children's well being and contribute to their school success.

- Each school must have financial, material, and programmatic resources adequate to provide each student an opportunity to learn to the highest standards established for the district, the state, or the nation. Measures of resource adequacy must take into account student characteristics, the cost of relevant effective practices, and geo-economic factors.
- Teachers and other educational professionals must have the commitment, knowledge, and skills to provide all students with an opportunity to learn to the highest established standards. This must include male and female students of diverse racial, ethnic, cultural, and linguistic backgrounds and those who are gifted and talented or have disabilities.
- Assessment and testing instruments and practices must be fair and unbiased, aligned with curricular content and learning opportunities, and used to inform instruction. They must not be used to foreclose students' opportunities to learn to the highest standards.

The absence of any one fundamental component of systemic reform can defeat any district or school's efforts to provide equitable, high quality education. Action to create and integrate them is needed at the federal, state, and local levels.

Source: Denbo, Grant, and Jackson, 1994, pp. 69–70.

Denbo, Grant, and Jackson (1994), the primary authors of the publication *Educate America: A Call for Equity in School Reform,* in which the Principles for Equity in Education appears (Box 2.1), end this list of principles with a call for action at the federal, state, and local levels.

Clearly, action at the state and federal levels has been taking place for many years and has been increasing in recent years. Likewise, a great deal of activity has been taking place at local levels, as educators have struggled to implement the provisions of their state accountability systems and of NCLB. However, these actions at all levels have not always been coherent, productive, or systematic, and there have been large problems with implementation and with unintended consequences of policies. Practitioners, frankly, need help in knowing how to proceed. In particular, they need help in knowing ways to proceed that will increase systemic equity in their schools and districts since that is what will be required to ultimately close achievement gaps.

CHAPTER CONCLUSION

We see the equity audits that are the topic of this book as providing the type of support educators, especially school and school system leaders, need in making a systemic response to reducing and eliminating achievement gaps. These audits are designed to be practical tools for practitioners to use in developing a better understanding of equity and inequity relationships in their current schools and districts. Also, these tools could be useful to professors in leadership preparation programs to help them develop future educational leaders who have the knowledge and skills they will need in the current high accountability context in U.S. public education.

For whoever is using these tools, though, it is important to understand that our concept of equity audits is a descendent of other versions of equity audits that have appeared in other arenas. *Equity audits* is a term that is used regularly in the United States and in international contexts. These audits are performed in a variety of educational and corporate settings to assess equity on a range of issues, including gender representation, access to health care, use of technology, and access to housing and public services. In the U.S. education arena specifically, equity audits have a history in at least three areas: (a) civil rights enforcement, (b) curriculum auditing and math/science reform, and (c) state accountability. We explore these histories in more detail in the next chapter.

DISCUSSION QUESTIONS AND ACTIVITIES

1. What does discussion of the concept of accountability typically sound like on your campus? Do teachers and administrators tend to focus on the national (i.e., NCLB) or your state's accountability requirements? Does your district or school have additional, local accountability measures? Do these discussions tend to be polarized along "good vs. bad" lines as was discussed in the first part of this chapter?

2. Do an Internet search for the Intercultural Development Research Association (IDRA) and investigate that organization's purpose and activities. How is Scott's definition of *systemic equity* aligned with this organization's mission?

3 History and Overview of Equity Audits

It is not only what we do, but also what we do not do, for which we are accountable.

—Moliere

The concept of equity audits that we present in this book is one that we have developed and refined to be used as a tool by school leadership practitioners. It is intended to help in their work to assess systemic equity in their schools and to assist them in planning for change. The term *equity audits*, however, is not something we invented. It is a phrase that has been used frequently with a variety of meanings in the United States and internationally in educational and corporate settings.

Equity audits also have a significant history in at least three areas of U.S. education. These areas include (a) civil rights enforcement, (b) curriculum auditing and math/science reform, and (c) state accountability. This chapter is included in the text for readers who are interested in the history, evolution, and context of the concept of equity auditing as we are using it. We first provide a context for the broader use of the term equity audits, and then we discuss the history of equity audits in U.S. education circles in more detail.

EQUITY AUDITS IN INTERNATIONAL PUBLIC AND PRIVATE SECTORS

Equity audits (also known as *representivity* audits) are commonplace in business, education, health care, and other settings in nations around the world. Corporations and government entities commonly conduct (or are subject to) employment equity audits, health equity audits, pay equity audits, gender equity audits, and technology equity audits, among others.

For example, England's Department of Health has developed a health equity audit for components of its National Health Service that includes a comprehensive self-assessment tool. This tool consists of statements and rating scales for health care providers to use in evaluating health inequalities for people of different population groups in England.

Another example of a governmental organization that utilizes equity audits is the New Zealand Department of Labor, which has developed a Pay and Employment Equity Audit focused on gender equity that "assess[es] the human resources policies and practices in each organization to check how free they are from gender bias" (New Zealand Department of Labor, 2006). The Department of Justice in Canada has conducted similar pay equity audits on public and private sector businesses.

In the education arena, the Australian Education Union, a union open to educators throughout Australia, has developed a version of equity audits they call the School Equity Audit. It contains a series of questions designed to assess the level of equal assess to school services for children from low-income homes (Box 3.1).

BOX 3.1

Example Items From School Equity Audit (Australian Education Union)

The purpose is to get teachers and principals to focus on "Barriers to Full Participation" in the policies of the school. The outcomes of the audit can be kept in the school and used for discussion.

1. Voluntary Fees

   1.1. Do you ask parents to donate voluntary fees to the school? How much?

   1.2. What measures do you take to encourage parents to pay them?

1.3. Do you think there are some parents that have difficulty affording these fees? How do you deal with this?

1.4. Are there students who feel embarrassed because their parents have not paid the fees?

1.5. Do other students know whose parents have and have not paid fees? How?

1.6. Do you stigmatize the students whose parents do not pay in any way?

1.7. Do you accept that there are some parents who cannot pay fees because they cannot afford them?

2. Excursions/School Camps/Other Extracurricular Expenditures

2.1. Have you in the past year or so had an off-site activity that involved the students paying?

2.2. What proportion of the eligible students went?

2.3. Do you think there were students who were not able to go because of the cost?

2.4. What arrangements were made for these students?

2.5. Does the school ever waive payment? How is this done? Do other students know?

3. Curriculum

3.1. Are there any activities within the normal school timetable that involve students paying? (e.g., for materials in a subject or course, including VET courses in secondary schools).

3.2. If yes, please give the subject/course.

3.3. Are there students who do not take these subjects because they cannot afford to?

3.4. Are there any arrangements which allow some of them to take the course anyway?

Source: Retrieved from the Australian Education Union Web site, www.aeufederal.org.au (direct link no longer available).

Though the title of the Australian Education Union's document is *School Equity Audit*, it focuses on only one aspect of equity in schools, that is, access to schooling for families with limited economic means.

EQUITY AUDITS IN U.S. EDUCATION

Civil Rights Enforcement

In the U.S. educational arena, formal, extensive equity audits of school districts are not uncommon. These are sometimes conducted voluntarily or result from pressure by local civic activists. In other cases they are ordered by the U.S. Department of Education, Office of Civil Rights as a way of determining the degree of compliance with a number of civil rights statutes that prohibit discrimination in educational programs and activities receiving federal funding. These statues include (a) Title VI of the Civil Rights Act of 1964 (prohibiting race, color, and national origin discrimination); (b) Title IX of the Education Amendments of 1972 (prohibiting sex discrimination); (c) Section 504 of the Rehabilitation Act of 1973 (prohibiting disability discrimination); (d) Title II of the Americans with Disabilities Act of 1990 (prohibiting disability discrimination by public entities); and (e) the Age Discrimination Act of 1975 (prohibiting age discrimination) (U.S. Department of Education, 1999, p. 1).

These types of equity audits focused on compliance with federal civil rights laws are extremely comprehensive, often producing reports on a single district that run several hundred pages. Such civil-rights-based equity audits are often performed by educational consultants who specialize in this work such as Harvard's Robert Peterkin. School districts around the country, including Urbana, Illinois; Ann Arbor, Michigan; Harrison, Colorado; and Albuquerque, New Mexico have had these extensive equity audits performed within the past ten years, and the results are available on the Internet.

Curriculum Auditing and Math/Science Reform

In addition to their use in the civil rights arena, equity audits have also been connected with curriculum audits, in a somewhat different way. In 1992, Jacqueline Mitchell and William Poston developed a version of school equity audits that was an adaptation of one standard area in comprehensive school curriculum audits (English, 1988).

Mitchell and Poston's (1992) version of equity audits drew from and expanded on curriculum audit Standard 3: "A School System Demonstrates Internal Connectivity and Rational Equity in its Program Development and Implementation." Poston (1992) proposed fifteen areas of analysis for use in equity audits (Box 3.2).

BOX 3.2

Poston's Areas of Analysis for Equity Audits

1. Administrative and supervisory practices

2. Course offerings and access

3. Financial and funding resources

4. Individual difference considerations

5. Materials and facilities

6. Special program and services delivery

7. Student management practices

8. Class-size practices

9. Demographic distribution

10. Grouping practices and instruction

11. Instructional time utilization

12. Promotion and retention practices

13. Staff development and training

14. Support services provision

15. Teacher assignment and work load

Source: Poston, 1992, p. 236.

Mitchell and Poston (1992) published one report of the application of this version of equity. It was a case study of three districts; we were not able to find additional published work using this method.

Another framework for analyzing school equity was developed by researchers studying math and science reform. Jane Kahle (1998) described what she called an *equity metric* based on her National Science Foundation funded work. She and her colleagues used this metric to study gender and racial equity in math and science in several schools (Hewson, Kahle, Scantlebury, & Davies, 2001). The categories in Hewson and colleagues' equity metric are shown in Box 3.3.

BOX 3.3

Kahle's Equity Indicators in Math and Science

Access

- Home resources
- Enrolled in algebra/geometry
- Expected academic program
- Limited English proficiency
- Quantity/quality of math/science courses

Retention

- Instructional quality
- Teacher expectations/behavior
- Teacher morale
- Teacher/student attitudes and beliefs
- Learning behavior
- Critical mass of students in science/mathematics class
- Student mobility
- Out-of-school experiences

Achievement

- Increase eighth grade math achievement
- Decrease "gap" between majority and minority students

Overall

- Equity plan
- Plan implemented
- Teacher mobility
- Administrator mobility
- Incentives for change/equity
- Quality of professional development
- Parental involvement

Source: Hewson et al., 2001, p. 1139.

The indicators in this equity metric for math and science include measures that would be easily assessable (test scores, student counts) along with measures that would be considerably more subjective and difficult to obtain (teacher expectations, out-of-school experiences).

STATE ACCOUNTABILITY

A third area in U.S. education in which equity audits have been used is state school reform and accountability efforts. In past years, several state departments of education developed instruments to evaluate equity levels in schools and school districts in their state, though these instruments varied widely in design. Kentucky's equity assessment instrument was in use until recently. It grew out of early work with curriculum audits in the state (Steffy, 1993) and has evolved and expanded through time.

The states of Washington and Iowa also formerly had state-level equity auditing and assessment processes. Washington's data was a based on a tool, and the Iowa Department of Education conducted onsite equity reviews of several school districts in the state each year. Both of these state-level equity assessment processes have now been discontinued.

REFINING EQUITY AUDITS
INTO A USABLE LEADERSHIP TOOL

Clearly, the general concept of equity audits has an important history both inside and outside of U.S. education settings. These streams of history for equity audits are the base on which we build our reframing of the concept into a useful school leadership tool. This reframing or refining is necessary because prior versions of equity audits (whether based on civil rights, curriculum auditing and math/science reform, or state accountability) have limited usability. Equity audits in the past have typically produced huge amounts of data that have tended to overwhelm decision makers. Although extremely detailed examinations of practices of schools and districts can be highly useful in some circumstances, such as documenting the violation of civil rights laws, they are not very useful in more practical, day-to-day leadership contexts. In our experience, few school leaders will have time or motivation to read through a several hundred-page document and then use the results well in planning school change.

In contrast, our concept of equity audits is a more focused, more limited descendent of earlier versions. School leaders need to have data for their schools and districts arranged in a clear and understandable way that reveals levels of equity and inequity in key areas. The results of these audits also need to be usable for planning and monitoring school change. Furthermore, state and federal accountability systems currently provide schools with enormous amount of data, but there is a major need for tools that will reduce some of the complexity of the data without stripping it of its utility for increasing equity.

Thus, for our version of equity audits, we suggest beginning with a manageable set of key indicators that together form a straightforward, delimited audit of equity. After careful consideration of the types of indicators available (from equity audits and from state accountability systems), we developed a model that has twelve indicators grouped into three areas: *programmatic equity, teacher quality equity, and achievement equity.* These three areas can even be conceptualized as a simple formula, as illustrated in Figure 3.1.

We should point out here that we understand clearly that at this point in the book many readers may be thinking that we are hopelessly naïve or completely unrealistic in proposing such a simplified (or what some might call simplistic) model. We do understand (and have said repeatedly here and elsewhere) that achieving educational equity is messily complex, emotional, and lifelong work.

However, in the schools we have studied and in our own work, we have learned that people have to begin this work somewhere. In other words, we all need a handle of manageable size to grasp onto. That is what we are after in presenting our streamlined version of equity audits in the first half of the book. Additionally, we deal with an additional portion of the complexity of educational equity work in the second half of the book where we turn to attitudes, beliefs, and strategies useful in addressing some of the inequities likely to be uncovered by the equity audit. We ask our readers to bear with us and to try to keep spaces open in their minds to consider what we propose.

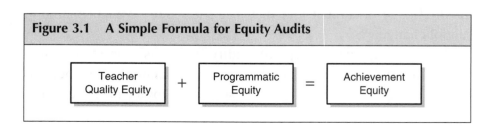

Figure 3.1   A Simple Formula for Equity Audits

Teacher Quality Equity + Programmatic Equity = Achievement Equity

SUGGESTED METHOD FOR CONDUCTING AN EQUITY AUDIT

We have used our version of equity audits for several years now, as have our colleagues in college courses and in schools and school districts around the country. Part of the power of our relatively unstructured model of equity audits is that practitioners have to make decisions about exactly how to do them based on local contextual factors—availability of data, school climate and culture, knowledge base of participants, and so forth. There is no spreadsheet or checklist that people could simply fill in that would satisfy the intent of this process. The power of this form of equity auditing is in the *process itself*—the process of making the choices about how to proceed, of gathering the data, of discussing the presentation of the results, of grappling with the meaning of what is revealed by the audit, and of planning for change.

However, we do want to suggest a basic process for using equity audits that readers could use as a guideline for customizing the work in their own schools and districts. This process is a simple one that has been used in many areas of organizational change and in applications of action research. In fact, this method for using equity audits could easily be incorporated into existing campus and/or district planning and decision-making processes, such as the site-based processes required in many states.

The first step is to put together a committee of relevant stakeholders, such as a group of teachers or a group that includes educators, parents, community members, business leaders, and/or students. It is important to identify individuals who are respected by the groups they represent and who are also people of good will who would be open to dialog and work focused on equity. Who, then, should be included? We would suggest influential teachers, especially representatives of teacher unions or other such groups; district and campus leaders; and representatives from parent and advocacy groups, such as Parent Teacher Association (PTA), Parent Teacher Organization (PTO), National Association for the Advancement of Colored People (NAACP), Mexican American Legal Defense and Education Fund (MALDEF), and so on. Student leaders could also be included at campuses that have students old enough to contribute meaningfully to the process.

Next, the available data for each of the areas the group wishes to audit should be presented to the group (or subgroups if conducting an audit in all three areas—teacher quality, programs, and achievement).

Furthermore, we would suggest presenting the data so that each committee member actually takes colored pencils, crayons, or markers and lays out the numbers or percentages on some graph paper that has been prepared for their use. Our experience has been that, though this takes a little time, actually "drawing" the percentages on graphs gives people a much better sense of the differences that need to be addressed.

The third step we suggest is for the committee to have an open discussion of equity gaps as they emerge. Experts could be brought in to offer analysis and advice. Educators from other districts that have had success in reducing teacher quality, program, or achievement gaps could be brought in for this step. Whoever is brought in to add to the discussion for this step needs to be a skillful facilitator. For example, issues of racism may be brought up at this point. Whatever comes up, though, needs to be addressed so that people perceive that they can say what they think and be heard by the other members of the committee, while at the same time the process must not be allowed to get stuck at some negative, nonproductive point that would prevent moving on to positive change. A good facilitator will know how to provide support for discussion of difficult issues and still also move the group forward in a positive way (see Sleeter, 1996, for an excellent discussion of how individuals and groups learn about racial and justice issues).

Our fourth step is that once there has been a good, open discussion of the problem, the group needs to move toward potential solutions. Again, experts or leadership from other schools or districts may be helpful here; similarly, a good facilitator will be useful in this phase. The point is to come up with some positive solutions; to talk about the strengths, weaknesses, and costs of each; and then to decide to commit to one or more of these solutions.

The fifth step is the implementation of the solution or solutions by the district. The sixth is to monitor results and then report them to the committee. If the solutions are successful, celebrate; if the solutions are not successful, return to either step three or four and work forward again. We would reiterate that many of the steps are already performed annually by schools and districts as part of campus and district planning. The equity audit could be incorporated in as part of these processes.

Here, then, are these same steps in a brief list:

Step 1: Create a committee of relevant stakeholders.

Step 2: Present the data to the committee and have everyone graph the data.

Step 3: Discuss the meaning of the data; possibly use experts or a facilitator.

Step 4: Discuss potential solutions, again possibly with outside assistance.

Step 5: Implement solution(s).

Step 6: Monitor and evaluate results.

Step 7: Celebrate if successful; if not successful, return to Step 3 and repeat the process.

CHAPTER CONCLUSION

In this chapter we have provided a history and overview of the concept of equity audits as well as suggested a simple process for conducting one. This information provides the background of earlier work on equity audits that lead to the development of the current form of equity audits that is the focus of our book and gives readers an example of a process that could be followed in conducting an equity audit in the areas covered by the next three chapters—teacher quality equity, programmatic equity, and achievement equity.

DISCUSSION QUESTIONS AND ACTIVITIES

1. How are U.S. public schools both like and unlike the other organizations and institutions that conduct equity audits as described in the first part of this chapter?

2. What would be the advantages and disadvantages of conducting a smaller, focused equity audit at your school (i.e., one focused on twelve indicators in three areas) versus a full-scale equity audit of the type that would be performed by the Office of Civil Rights?

3. Try an Internet search of your own for the phrase "equity audits" and see where the concept is in use in the United States and in international settings.

Part II

The Equity Audit Process for Schools and Districts

4 Teacher Quality Equity

In the last ten years there's been a lot of research done about what makes a difference for student achievement, and it's now clear that the single most important determinant of what students learn is what their teachers know. Teacher qualifications, teachers' knowledge and skills, make more difference for student learning than any other single factor.

—Linda Darling-Hammond

Access to high quality teachers is one of the key factors at the school level that influences student achievement, a point on which there is a remarkable level of agreement among educational researchers, policy makers, and practitioners (Cohen & Hill, 2000, 2001; Darling-Hammond, 1999; Ferguson, 1998; Heck, 2007). Specifying exactly what teacher quality is and determining how it should be measured, of course, is a much more complicated issue (Rowan, Correnti, & Miller, 2002).

The framers of NCLB, for example, defined teacher quality in particular ways in the policy provisions pertaining to "highly qualified teachers." According to NCLB, highly qualified teachers are those who (1) have full certification or licensure, (2) hold a college degree, and (3) have demonstrated content knowledge in all the subjects they teach (Smith, Desimone, & Ueno, 2005). Schools, school districts, and states are held accountable under NCLB for ensuring that all students have access to highly qualified teachers under this federal definition.

Individual states have also chosen to address student access to quality teachers in specific ways. The state of Tennessee, for example, has developed the Tennessee Value Added Assessment System (TVAAS) based on a statistical estimation of the contribution each teacher makes to students' standardized test performance based on each student's prior achievement (for more information, see https://tvaas.sas.com/evaas/public_welcome.jsp). The Tennessee model has attracted national attention, and there has been considerable discussion among researchers and practitioners about the benefits and challenges of using such models (e.g., Ballou, Sanders, & Wright, 2004; Doran & Fleischman, 2005; McCaffrey, Lockwood, Koretz, Louis, & Hamilton, 2004; Raudenbush, 2004).

For instance, research based on the Tennessee model has shown strong and additive detrimental effects for children assigned to the least effective teachers for several elementary grades in a row (Prince, 2002; Sanders & Rivers, 1996). However, this model has also been subject to considerable critique based on methodological concerns (Bock & Wolfe, 1996; McCaffrey et al., 2004) and concerns about the narrowness of its definition of teacher quality (one based completely on gain scores on standardized tests). For these reasons and also because the use of such models requires high quality longitudinal data systems that many states do not yet have, other states have been slow to adopt value added accountability systems.

Thus, other measures that are more readily assessable and that can serve as proxies for direct measures of teacher quality (such as experience and training) are more commonly used by state accountability systems and, as noted earlier, by NCLB (Rowan, Correnti, & Miller, 2002). Whatever definition of teacher quality that we use, however, there is considerable evidence that student access to high quality teachers is usually *not* distributed on an equitable basis to all students within individual schools, particularly high schools. Students of color and students from low-income homes more often have teachers with less experience, with less education and training, and without certification (Ingersoll, 1999; Lankford, Loeb, & Wyckoff, 2002).

The purpose of the equity audit in the area of teacher quality, then, is to examine how teacher quality is distributed *within a particular school*. That is, school data on four indicators of teacher quality are evaluated using the equity audit to see which children are being taught by which teachers in what subjects or content areas.

Specifically, for our version of equity audits, we have chosen four indicators for which data are commonly available (from the state, school district, or local campus) and for which there is research showing effects on student achievement (Rice, 2003; Rowan, Correnti, & Miller, 2002): (1) teacher education (college degrees), (2) teacher experience (years working as a teacher), (3) teacher mobility (teachers changing campuses annually), and (4) teacher certification (teachers assigned in or out of area of teaching expertise). The central question in all four of these areas is to what degree are they distributed equitably or inequitably across grade levels, classes, and student groups within a school. For example, do classes serving English language learners, special education students, or basic-level mathematics courses have the same percentage of teachers holding master's degrees or higher, the same percentage of experienced teachers, the same percentage of teacher mobility rate, and the same percentage of uncertified teachers and teachers teaching outside their areas as classes serving gifted and talented students, general education students, and advanced mathematics classes?

We understand that some educators would argue that individual teachers, especially "senior" teachers (senior by experience, degree, or status), have autonomy and often choose the highest-level classes within a school, and therefore, the school leadership does not have much control over this. This is precisely the point that this teacher quality dimension of the equity audit is intended to challenge. In our research and practice, we have worked with many schools that have challenged and subsequently changed their "seniority" assumptions about which teachers should (or are automatically entitled) to teach which classes and which students. Furthermore, the first step toward making such changes is getting an accurate picture of the current situation with respect to distribution of teacher quality indicators on a campus.

TEACHER EDUCATION

To begin to show how the equity audit in the teacher quality dimension works, let's begin with the indicator for teacher education. Research has shown that the amount of content knowledge a teacher has about her or his subject area is related to how much her or his students learn (Hill, Rowan, & Ball, 2005). Though the type of college degree a teacher has is not a direct measure of how much content expertise that teacher has, it can serve as a proxy indicator for how much education in course content a teacher has received. The central question for the equity audit in the area of teacher education, though, is the relative distribution of such expertise across a single campus. For example, some campuses will have many teachers with masters' degrees and a few with doctorates. Other campuses will have very few teachers holding advanced degrees. Regardless of whether a campus has many or few teachers with advanced degrees, it is important to get an accurate picture of how the resource these teachers represent is being utilized by the school.

The typical situation for schools that have not systematically examined the distribution of teacher quality indicators (including teacher education) within their school is that the teachers who hold advanced degrees in their content areas will be clustered in the per-ceived "higher-level" or more prestigious teaching assignments. Depending on the type of campus, this can mean higher-level sec-tions in schools that use ability grouping; gifted and talented, advanced, honors, pre-Advanced Placement (Pre-AP), Advanced Placement (AP), or International Baccalaureate (IB) classes or sec-tions; or courses or sections that are at the top end of a sequential curriculum, such as physics or calculus.

We should be clear here that we are not saying that teachers who hold advanced degrees in their subjects should not teach the higher-end courses. What we are saying is that to equitably distribute the resource these teachers represent across a campus, teachers with advanced degrees should not *only* teach upper-division courses. All students should have equal opportunity to learn from the most highly qualified teachers on campus.

For example, Ms. Brown, who holds a master's degree in physics, might be given a schedule, such as the one in Table 4.1, that shows her teaching not only Advanced Placement Physics but also freshman-level physical science.

TEACHER EXPERIENCE

As was true about the indicator for teacher education, teacher experience is also related to student achievement. Research shows this

Table 4.1	Example Equitable Teacher Schedule					
	Period 1	Period 2	Period 3	Period 4	Period 5	Period 6
Brown, J. A.	Physical Science	Physical Science	Planning	Physics I	Physics I	AP Physics I

to be the case (Rockoff, 2004), but it also intuitively makes sense for most educators that teachers progress through stages as they gain experience in the classroom, increasingly becoming more proficient at management and routine, problem solving, student relations, and instructional strategies (Berliner, 2001).

For the purposes of the equity audit, however, the central question is, again, the *distribution* of teacher experience across the range of instructional settings on any particular campus. Some schools will have greater numbers of highly experienced teachers and other schools will have fewer, but it is the patterns of assignment of the teachers within a school that can determine equitable or inequitable access to the resource of experienced teachers among different student groups.

As was the case with the teacher education indicator discussed earlier, teacher experience on campuses that have not systematically evaluated levels of equity or inequity present at that school is most often unevenly distributed with the most experienced teachers assigned to teach the perceived *top*-level classes and students. For this area of the equity audit, we will use as an example (Table 4.2) data from an actual school that has addressed this common area of inequitable distribution in teacher quality and has deliberately spread out its experienced teachers in all levels of mathematics.

Shown in Table 4.2 is a section of the master schedule for an actual high school that serves a highly diverse student population for the 2007–2008 school year. Clearly there is a balance of the most experienced and least experienced teachers teaching all levels of mathematics at this school. Although our example school is to be commended for this achievement, it is important to point out that this would not be the typical result for an equity audit of the distribution of teacher experience in most U.S. high schools.

Table 4.2	An Atypical High School Math Department		
Teacher #	Department	Subjects Taught	Years Experience
1	MATH	ALG I	0–5
2	MATH	ALG II; MATH MODELS	over 10
3	MATH	GEOM	over 10
4	MATH	ALG II; MATH MODELS	over 10
5	MATH	GEOM	over 10
6	MATH	ALG II; MATH MODELS	over 10
7	MATH	ALG II; EXIT TEST PREP	6–10 yrs
8	MATH	AB CALCULUS	0–5
9	MATH	ALG III	over 10
10	MATH	ALG I	over 10
11	MATH	BC CALC; GEOM; DEPT CHAIR	6–10 yrs
12	MATH	GEOM	6–10 yrs
13	MATH	ALG II	over 10
14	MATH	MATH MODELS; EXIT TEST PREP	0–5
15	MATH	PRECAL; STAT; IB	over 10
16	MATH	ALG I SUPPORT	over 10
17	MATH	GEOM	0–5
18	MATH	ALG I	0–5
19	MATH	PRECAL	over 10
20	MATH	ALG I; LEAD ALG I	6–10 yrs
21	MATH	ALG I	0–5
22	MATH	PRECAL; ALG II	over 10
23	MATH	ALG I	6–10 yrs
24	MATH	GEOM; ALG II	6–10 yrs
25	MATH	ALG II EXIT TEST PREP	over 10
26	MATH	ALG I	6–10 yrs

TEACHER MOBILITY

Teacher mobility, like the teacher quality indicators discussed in the previous two sections, has been linked by research to systematic differences in student performance (Lankford, Loeb, & Wyckoff, 2002).

The reason for this is also something that is easy for experienced educators to predict and to understand. Whenever a teacher changes campuses, there is a learning curve period that takes place while the teacher learns to be effective and comfortable operating in a new system of routines and procedures and a new campus culture. Furthermore, as campuses implement programs and training to address student instructional needs, they typically invest considerable resources in teacher training and professional development. Every time a teacher who has had such training leaves, and a new one takes her or his place, it is necessary to train the new teacher, and valuable knowledge walks out the door with the departing teacher.

It is not hard to see how campuses with extremely high turnover rates for teachers find it virtually impossible to plan, implement, and sustain change. Additionally, it is the very campuses that face the most significant educational challenges that have the highest teacher mobility rates (Fuller & Berry, 2006). Once again, though, in considering this indicator for the equity audit, the focus should be concerning how teacher turnover might differentially affect programs, grade levels, and groups of students on a campus. The issue here is simply, where are the teachers *new to this campus* (who may or may not be new to teaching) assigned?

Table 4.3 shows a typical situation for an elementary school that uses ability grouping to assign students to teachers (the *A* section of each grade level is the highest ability group; the *D* section is the lowest). The teachers newest to the campus cluster in the (perceived) lower-ability sections at each grade level.

Due to assumptions of privilege associated with seniority at a campus, teachers who have been in a building longer may have a sense of entitlement to teach the *upper* sections at any particular grade level, an assumption that may be unspoken but nonetheless supported by the existing campus culture. Thus, the teachers newest to campus—the ones who may not have had the professional development needed for programs in place at the school, the ones who are having to learn a new environment, and the ones who may be new to teaching altogether—are always assigned to the students who have the greatest learning needs.

TEACHER CERTIFICATION

The fourth indicator in the equity audit dimension of teacher quality is teacher certification. Like the other three indicators for this dimension of the audit, teacher certification influences how well students learn

Table 4.3 Teacher Mobility in Example Elementary School	
Class	*Teacher Years Experience at This Campus*
3A	12
3B	15
3C	2
3D	0
4A	5
4B	5
4C	0
4D	1
5A	10
5B	8
5C	2
5D	3

content. Teacher certification is similar to but not identical to teacher education. In other words, it is possible to have an appropriately degreed teacher in a classroom but to have that teacher lack the proper certification for the particular subject or content area she or he is assigned to teach. For example, a teacher may be degreed and certified to teach general elementary school classes but be assigned to teach English as a Second Language (ESL) classes for which he or she is not certified.

This problem is particularly acute in the so-called "high need" areas of teacher certification, including special education, bilingual education, mathematics, science, and technology. And as with other areas of teacher quality, the schools perceived to be the most challenging ones in which to teach—rural, urban, and those serving majority children of color and low-income populations—are the schools that have the highest concentrations of uncertified teachers and teachers teaching outside of their certification areas (Darling-Hammond, 1999).

Additionally, some subject areas are perennially considered high-need areas because of the difficulty in recruiting, hiring, and retaining certified teachers. For example, Figure 4.1 shows the percentage of newly hired teachers statewide in Texas for the 2000–2001 school year that *were not fully certified for the positions* for which they were hired.

For the campus-level equity audit, however, the central issue is yet again the distribution within the campus of teachers who are not certified or who are teaching outside the areas for which they hold certification. The typical situation is that the courses and students perceived to be those at the highest level are staffed by appropriately certified teachers, while at the same time the courses and students perceived to be at the lowest level have most of the uncertified or inappropriately certified teachers.

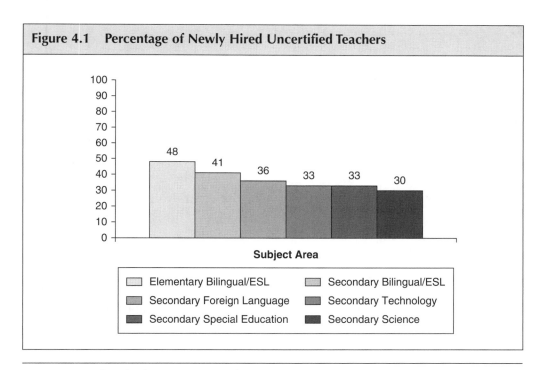

Figure 4.1   Percentage of Newly Hired Uncertified Teachers

Source: Institute for School-University Partnerships, 2001.

CHAPTER CONCLUSION

Taken together, these four indicators of teacher quality—teacher education, teacher experience, teacher turnover, and teacher certification—can show a clear and easily understandable picture of patterns of equitable or inequitable access to the most qualified teachers on a particular campus for different groups of students. Furthermore, we would suggest that campuses using the equity audit should gather data for multiple years on the teacher quality indicators to allow better understanding of the patterns through time on differential access to qualified teachers. In other words, almost any campus can have a single year in which circumstances force less-than-ideal teacher assignment decisions, but it is a different situation altogether if the same patterns of inequity occur year after year.

Furthermore, it is unrealistic to expect such patterns to spontaneously change in the absence of planful intervention on the part of school leaders and the school community. It is equally unrealistic to expect large improvements in student achievement or great narrowing in achievement gaps on a campus if certain groups of students routinely and persistently are taught by the least qualified, newest teachers on a campus year after year.

DISCUSSION QUESTIONS AND ACTIVITIES

1. If you wanted to conduct an equity audit for your campus in the area of teacher quality, where would you go to get the data? Is this information kept and tracked systematically on your campus? Would you have to go to the district central office? Would either the campus or the central office have the data in usable form, or would someone have to go through individual personnel files? If the data are not readily available, why not? Would the data be released to you if you asked for it at either the campus or district levels?

2. Suppose your campus conducted an equity audit in the area of teacher quality and learned that teacher mobility is high for your campus and that new teachers and teachers new to your campus are inequitably distributed across grades and teaching assignments. Why, specifically, could this result in learning inequities on your campus? What programs (curriculum, instruction, discipline, technology, student success, and so on) are in place on your campus for which new teachers might have to wait for professional development or for which training is no longer provided? What specific contextual factors are present at your school that more experienced teachers have grown accustomed to that cause difficulties for new teachers? Does your campus have a coherent plan for addressing any of these issues?

5 Programmatic Equity

It is one thing to take as a given that approximately 70 percent of an entering high school freshman class will not attend college, but to assign a particular child to a curriculum designed for that 70 percent closes off for that child the opportunity to attend college.

—James Coleman

The second component area of the equity audit is *programmatic equity*. In this area we will be focusing on the quality of the educational programs (i.e., instructional settings) into which students are placed or from which they are excluded. Though it may make many of us educators uncomfortable to admit it, there are huge variations in quality among different programs within the same schools (see Schoenfeld, 2002, for an excellent discussion of differences in quality of math programs). Among different student groups within schools, there are also typically systematic differences in access to programs.

Obviously, there are a great variety of programs in most schools, so the number of *potential* indicators in this component of the equity audit is quite large. However, in order to stick with a manageable set of four indicators for each category, we've selected four key program areas that research consistently has shown to be likely sites for inequity. These four are (a) special education, (b) gifted and talented education (G/T), (c) bilingual education, and (d) student discipline.

SPECIAL EDUCATION

The over-assignment of students from certain groups, particularly African American males, to special education has long been recognized as a problem of gross inequity with U.S. schools (Artiles, 1998; Losen & Orfield, 2002; MacMillan & Reschy, 1998). Though recognition of the problem has existed for decades, the patterns of high placement rates for African Americans, particularly boys, in special education generally and in certain, severe disability categories such as mental retardation and emotionally disturbed, specifically, continue to the present day.

Additionally, the current U.S. policy context of high-stakes accountability systems complicates the problem by increasing the pressure on educators to raise student performance for all groups. There is concern that this pressure may encourage over-identification of students for special education in order to qualify them for special testing (Texas Center for Educational Research, 2000; Townsend, 2002).

The question to be addressed for this indicator of the equity audit, then, is do the participation rates in special education for various groups of students on an individual campus match the overall proportional representation of these same groups in the school population as a whole? Table 5.1 shows real 2007 data for a Texas school and illustrates large inequity in special education placement rates.

In this example school, not only are African American students *over*represented in special education at 158% of what would be proportional to their representation in the overall student population, Hispanic students are *under*represented by almost one third of what would be proportional. Both these situations are potentially problematic for the

Table 5.1	Representation of Student Groups in Special Education and General Population		
Student Group	*Percentage of School Population*	*Percentage of Special Education Population*	*Difference*
African American	24	38	+14
Hispanic	42	30	−12
White	34	32	−2

school. Students in one group (African American) may be being placed in special education inappropriately, and students in the other group (Hispanic) may not be receiving special education services that they might legitimately qualify for and need.

GIFTED AND TALENTED

The problem of too many students from certain groups receiving placement in special education settings is reversed in the area of gifted and talented education (G/T) (Ford & Harmon, 2001). Specifically, students from low-income homes and students of color are identified as gifted and talented at rates far lower than their proportional representation in the general student population. This pattern is prevalent in schools and school districts across the United States. Thus, the indicator for the equity audit in the G/T area is whether or not students from all groups are served through G/T in percentages appropriate to their group's representation in the school. In other words, if 30% of students at a particular campus are African American students, then 30% of students identified and served through the gifted and talented program should be African American.

Table 5.2 shows actual data for the entire state of Texas for the 2004–2005 school year for placement in G/T programs, disaggregated by race. It is clear to see from the statewide data (highly likely to be mirrored on most individual campuses) that African American and Hispanic students are greatly underrepresented in G/T classes, while white students and Asian students are overrepresented. Native American students are the only student group that is close to proportional representation. This is an inequity pattern that is a substantial hindrance to the removal of achievement gaps.

BILINGUAL EDUCATION

The third area under programmatic equity considered by the equity audit is bilingual education (or English as a Second Language, or English for Speakers of Other Languages). This is an important area to consider under programmatic equity because ever-increasing numbers of students whose home language is not English enroll in U.S. schools each year. Regrettably, our schools do not have a very good track record

Table 5.2	Texas K–8, 2004–2005, Identified Gifted/Talented by Race/Ethnicity				
Race/ Ethnicity	Number Enrolled	Percentage of Total Population	Number of Identified G/T	Percentage of Total G/T Population	Percentage Difference Between Total Population and G/T Population
Native American	9,971	0.33	645	0.29	–0.04
Asian	88,796	3	13,494	6	+3
African American	415,980	14	19,372	9	–5
Anglo	1,103,979	37	113,352	51	+14
Hispanic	1,360,536	46	74,761	34	–12
Total	2,979,262	100.33	221,624	100.29	

Source: Texas Education Agency, 2005.

in terms of providing quality education for English language learners. Bilingual programs all too often have been low-expectation settings into which students were segregated where they did not learn English at the level needed for on-grade-level academic progress and where they did not progress in their first language either (Moll, 1992).

In response to this typical situation in bilingual education, states have begun reporting accountability data separately for students served through bilingual education or other programs designed for students learning English. Typical measures in this include reporting of state achievement test data separately for English language learners, test data for achievement tests given in home languages (e.g., Spanish), and sometimes measures of progress toward mastery of English.

As Black and Valenzuela (2003) pointed out, however, caution is in order in selecting and evaluating data about bilingual programs. In other words, learning English should not be the only legitimate outcome of bilingual programs. Equally important are program goals such as proficiency and literacy in students' home languages and valuing and preserving students' home cultures. In fact, local school administrators reported using a variety of data sources to evaluate and make decisions about the effectiveness of bilingual programs in research conducted by Gates and Lichtenberg (2005). These measures are shown in Box 5.1.

BOX 5.1

Data Sources Used to Evaluate Bilingual Education Programs

- State achievement test
- Oral language testing
- English norm-referenced testing
- Spanish norm-referenced testing
- Retention rates
- High school status of "on track to graduate"
- Student socioeconomic status (SES)
- Attendance
- Student mobility
- Student discipline
- Report card grades

Source: Gates & Lichtenberg, 2005.

DISCIPLINE

The fourth area under programmatic equity focused on by the equity audit is discipline. Though this may seem somewhat odd when considered alongside the other three areas (special education, gifted and talented education, and bilingual education), it is nonetheless a critically important area. The reason discipline is such an important area to consider in the equity audit is that students who are involved in the discipline system at their schools are frequently removed from their regular classes and do not have the same access to learning as their peers who are not considered "discipline problems." We would argue that, for some students (particularly African American and Latino boys), the disciplinary settings on their campuses become their instructional placement since that is where they spend most of their time.

To illustrate, Figure 5.1 shows actual disciplinary data for a high school of 1,300 students. At this school, African American males received disciplinary action (in all categories from minor infractions to expulsion combined) at a rate that is nearly *three times* the rate that would be proportional with their representation in the general school population. For Latino boys, the rate is *more than four times* what would be proportional.

Clearly, this high school has serious inequity in its disciplinary actions, as equity audits of many schools nationwide also would show

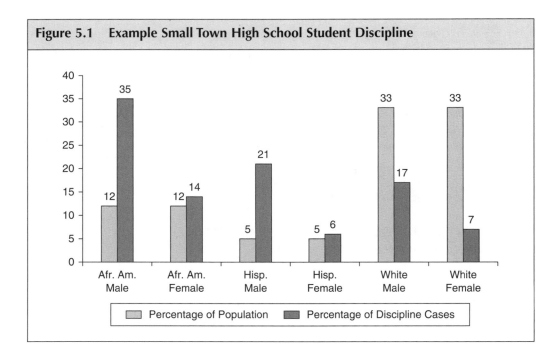

Figure 5.1   Example Small Town High School Student Discipline

to be the case (Bowman, 2003; Gregory, 1995). As a result of this inequitable situation, African American and Latino boys at this school spend much less time in their regular classrooms, and thus, have differential opportunities to learn the curriculum.

CHAPTER CONCLUSION

We have presented four programmatic equity areas—special education, gifted and talented education, bilingual education, and discipline—that we suggest as key indicators to be considered by educators conducting equity audits of their schools. We understand that many educators might want to argue that the inequities in these areas are somehow produced by nature or by society and that we educators can do little to change them. We would and are arguing just the opposite—that these inequities are in large part produced by the systems in place in our schools. It is our attitudes, assumptions, and practices that produce the data we see in these areas, and those things are all within our control and can be changed. Furthermore, we have changed these things ourselves as practitioners; we have students in our classes who are changing them in their schools; and we have studied schools as researchers that have changed them. The first step in all of these changes for all of these people has been a willingness to face the current situation of inequity and to accept ownership of the problem (see Rorrer, Skrla, & Scheurich, 2008).

DISCUSSION QUESTIONS AND ACTIVITIES

1. Walk through the halls of your campus and through the areas where students wait for disciplinary action and to which they are assigned discipline consequences. Based just on your observations, do you think the students who are outside of their regular classes for disciplinary reasons are representative of your school's general pupil population? If you asked a colleague to conduct a similar walk around focused on the same question, do you think she or he would reach the same conclusion that you did? What would an equity audit of this indicator likely show for your school?

2. Do you know the procedures for identifying students as G/T at your school? If not, obtain a copy of the guidelines for identification, service, and exit for G/T students at your campus. Review these procedures in light of what an equity audit for your campus in this area would likely reveal.

3. If your school assembled a team to conduct an equity audit for your school, would you include students on the team? If so, why? If not, why not? At what age might students be able to contribute significantly as part of an equity audit team? Who else do you think should be involved—parents, community members, support staff, business leaders?

6 Achievement Equity

If states were closing achievement gaps on their own, the federal government would not have needed to intervene.

—William Taylor

Without a doubt, student achievement equity is the category of the equity audit that has and continues to receive the most scrutiny and attention from the public, media, policy makers, researchers, and practitioners. No Child Left Behind (NCLB) and its reauthorization have ensured that the U.S. national spotlight has remained focused on student achievement. Thus, we have appropriately included it as the third main category of our version of equity audits. We do, however, wish to widen the spotlight beyond the usual attention to state achievement test results to examine other indicators of student achievement and attainment.

The reason for including areas other than state achievement tests in the equity audit for achievement equity is that we have learned from our research (Skrla & Scheurich, 2001; Skrla, Scheurich, & Johnson, 2000; Skrla, Scheurich, & Johnson, 2001; Skrla, Scheurich, Johnson, & Koschoreck, 2001a, 2001b) that equitable achievement on relatively low-level state tests is not *true* achievement equity when large gaps remain on other, higher-level measures of student performance. Thus, a broader definition of achievement equity is needed, and the four indicators we include in the achievement equity category of the equity audit include (a) state achievement tests, (b) dropout rates, (c) high school graduation tracks, and (d) SAT/ACT/AP/IB results.

STATE ACHIEVEMENT TESTS

All 50 states now give achievement tests and are required by NCLB to publish disaggregated results by family income status, race, disability, and English proficiency, though not by gender. Student performance on these state assessments is the primary national accountability measure and features prominently in state accountability systems, so state test scores are the first indicator area for achievement equity. Although there is wide disparity on the approach states have taken to developing their state assessment systems, all states have methods of reporting the results to schools, parents, and the public and of assigning ratings to schools based, at least in part, on these tests.

The reason that the area of state achievement test results still needs a careful focus area for those conducting an equity audit, however, is not a lack of available data. It is that at the campus level, there is often a lack of meaningful analysis of what these data show about a particular school in terms of equity or inequity. In other words, schools these days many times are data rich but are analysis poor.

Our example school (Figure 6.1) for this area of programmatic equity is another positive one. This shows the progress of different student groups over multiple years on a state reading exam. This

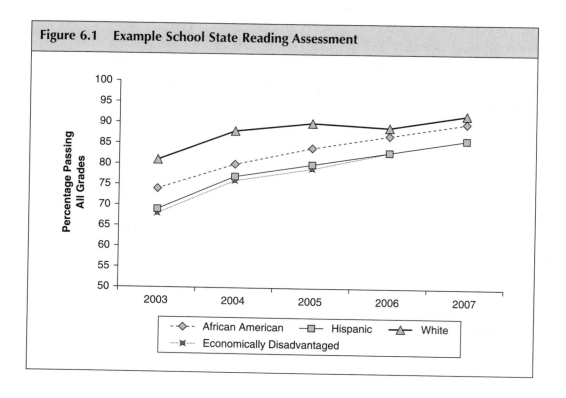

Figure 6.1   Example School State Reading Assessment

school has conducted an equity audit and has used the results to make changes in programs and policies to target achievement gaps.

DROPOUT RATES

High school dropout rates, or school completion rates, are another key indicator to be considered for the equity audit. Concern about grossly inequitable and unacceptable dropout rates is increasingly and justifiably at the forefront of educational policy debates in the United States (Haney, 2001). It is unfortunately all too typical for less than half of students in some student groups (e.g., Latino boys) to finish high school with their peers (Education Trust, 2006).

Unfortunately, reliable data about exactly how severe this problem is has been difficult to come by as there are a variety of means for calculating dropout rates, and some states systems for doing so seem to obscure more than they reveal about who is actually earning a regular high school diploma. This has improved somewhat since the advent of NCLB, however, and most educators should be able to have access to data that will show dropout and/or school completion numbers for their campus. We would also say here that middle schools and elementary schools should not skip this step in the equity audit because the factors that cause students to drop out before finishing high school (below grade-level achievement, chronic discipline issues, disengagement with school) begin while students are in elementary school and intensify in middle school (Wehlage & Rutter, 1986). Thus, elementary, intermediate, middle, and junior high schools should consider the graduation rates at the campuses in their feeder patterns as part of their equity audits.

Figure 6.2 shows real data from an urban high school for the percentage of students in each group who complete high school with a diploma. Clearly, this school is moving in the wrong direction in this area of the equity audit.

GRADUATION TRACKS

The third area to be considered by the equity audit under the category of achievement equity is high school graduation tracks. It is important to analyze data in this area because all students who graduate from high school may not have the opportunity to master equally demanding curricula. That is, many states offer some form of basic,

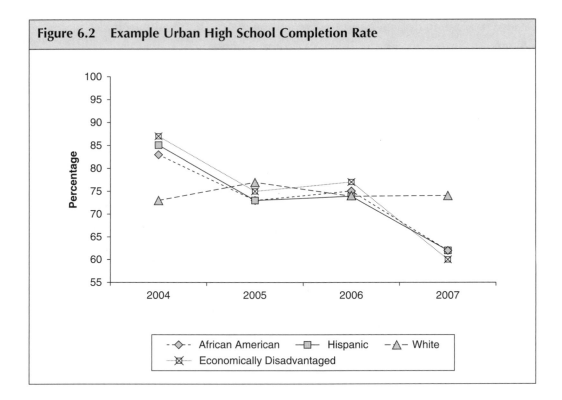

Figure 6.2 **Example Urban High School Completion Rate**

intermediate, advanced, and/or college preparatory diplomas. The central question to be addressed by this indicator is whether students in each racial and Student Socioeconomic Status (SES) group earn each type of diploma in proportions similar to their representation in the general population of the school.

In other words, if 40% of students at a particular high school earn the top-level diploma, what is the racial and SES makeup of that 40% in relation to the total school population? The reason it is so important to consider this area in the audit is that children of color and those from low-income homes are typically found in the college track at much, much lower numbers than are white children and children from middle- and upper-income homes (Oakes, 1986; Sizer, 1997; Wheelock, 1993).

Figure 6.3 provides an example of this type of inequity.

SAT/ACT/AP/IB PERFORMANCE

The fourth and final area to be addressed by the equity audit in the achievement equity category is performance on the SAT, the ACT, AP,

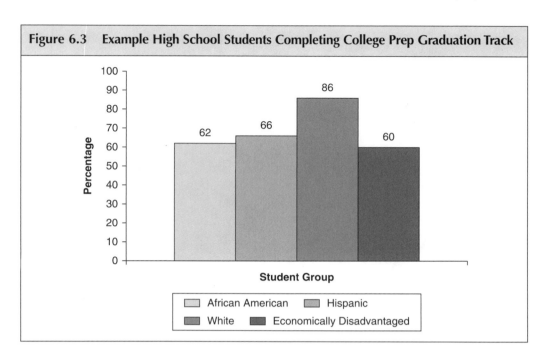

Figure 6.3   Example High School Students Completing College Prep Graduation Track

and/or IB examinations. As was the case for the other indicators we have discussed in this category, students of color and students from low-income homes most often score lower on these tests than do white students and students from middle- and upper-income homes. Furthermore, in addition to examining the scores on the tests themselves, examination of participation rates is also important because students of color and students from low-income homes many times do not even take the preparatory classes or the tests themselves (College Board, 2001).

For example, Figure 6.4 shows actual 2007 data from an urban high school for student performance on Advanced Placement exams. For this school, the gaps among different student groups are very large on both percentage of the group tested and percentage meeting the minimum criterion for earning college credit on the exams. More than four times as many white students take AP exams than do African American students.

CHAPTER CONCLUSION

We have identified four key areas of achievement equity—state test scores, dropout rates, graduation tracks, and SAT/ACT/AP/IB scores—to be examined by those conducting equity audits for their

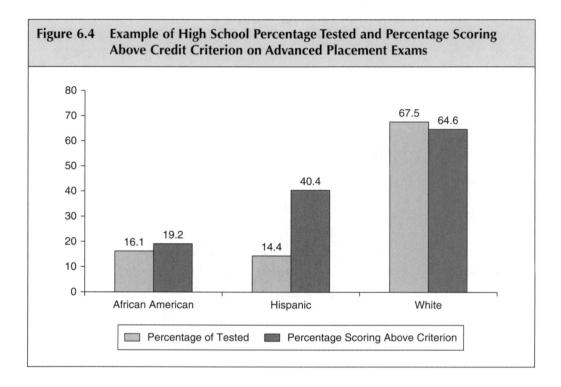

Figure 6.4   Example of High School Percentage Tested and Percentage Scoring Above Credit Criterion on Advanced Placement Exams

campuses. We realize that is yet another area in which the first reaction of many educators will be to say that the inequities revealed by this equity audit category are due to innate differences, societal factors, or individual decisions by students and/or their families. All these things are beyond the control of educators. Certainly, some of these external factors may influence what the equity audit reveals about a school in the area of achievement equity. Nonetheless, our lived experience, our research, and the research of others (beginning notably with Edmonds, 1979) shows us clearly that there is much to be done with respect to improving equity in these areas that *is within the control* of educators and that substantial, sustained progress can be achieved.

DISCUSSION QUESTIONS AND ACTIVITIES

1. Let's say you have reviewed state assessment data for the students on your campus and the equity audit revealed substantial inequities between the performance of students from low-income homes and those from middle- and upper-income homes. What process could you use on your campus to develop a plan to identify and address the flaws in your current system?

Does your school develop an annual campus improvement plan? Are there other campus structures or committees in place that would be likely sites to begin the work to change these achievement inequities?

2. If you are at a high school, compare the student enrollments of your ninth grades and twelfth grades over the past three years. Are these figures in line with what your school officially reports as an annual dropout rate? If they are not, where do you think the missing students actually go? How could your campus begin to gather more accurate data on students who fail to complete school if this is needed?

7 Equity Audits at the School District Level

The strength of our nation depends on the strength of our schools, especially those in large urban districts that serve so many of our children.

—Eli Broad

Up to this point in this book, we have concentrated our discussion of equity audits at the individual campus level. We chose this approach for two reasons. First, most of the interaction we have had with practitioners around our earlier, article-length version of equity audits was with principals, directors of instruction, and others at the campus level who were working to change campuses. Second, the individual campus is properly the site of ground-level action to change what happens between teachers and students, and thus, to change in a positive way student outcomes.

Nonetheless, we clearly realize that there is also a role for district-level leadership in conducting equity audits. We and other scholars have done a great deal of research, in fact, that focuses on the school district role in improving achievement and advancing equity (Rorrer, Skrla, & Scheurich, 2008). However, for the equity audit at the school district level, a somewhat different focus is required, and that is what we discuss in this chapter.

At the district level, there is essentially one large question: Do systematic differences exist across campuses within the same district on the indicators of the equity audit? That is, no matter what the overall level of performance for the district is on a particular indicator, are there campuses that differ substantially from the district mean, and are these differences associated with the racial and economic composition of the campuses?

Mitchell and Poston (1992), in their conceptualization of equity audits, suggested that campuses that differed from district averages by more than 20% were likely indicators of district inequity. In our earlier work on equity audits, we suggested that raising this standard (to a 10% deviation from the district average) would be more likely to leverage equity within a district.

Figure 7.1 shows an example of this principle using actual 2007 data from a suburban school district. For this example district, the average campus percentage of students considered economically disadvantaged is 31%. The district average of teachers with between one and five years of teaching experience is 34%, and the district average for teachers with between eleven and twenty years experience is 21%. Using our 10% deviation standard, any campus that has more than 37% of teachers with one to five years experience or less than 19% of teachers with 11–20 years experience would be campuses to look more

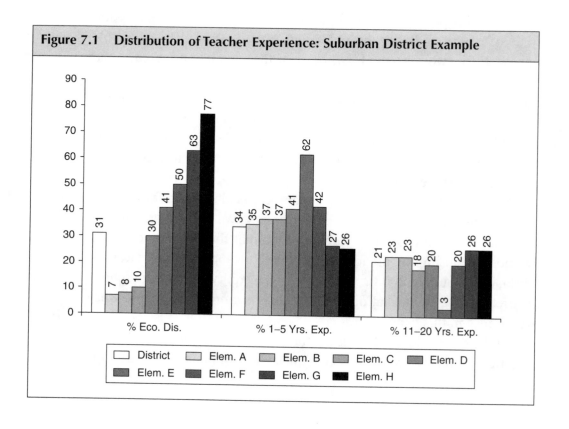

Figure 7.1   Distribution of Teacher Experience: Suburban District Example

closely at in the area of teacher assignment. Three campuses (D, E, & F) would meet this standard for possibly having too many inexperienced teachers, and two campuses (C & E) would meet it for potentially having too few experienced teachers. Clearly, from this illustration, Elementary School E would be the one most in need of district scrutiny (and assistance) regarding teacher assignment.

The same principle of looking for 10% or greater deviation from district averages would apply in all areas of the equity audit: teacher quality equity, programmatic equity, and student achievement equity. The direction of the deviation that would trigger district action would be determined by the nature of the indicator. For example, having 10% fewer than the district average African American males assigned to special education would be a very positive sign for a campus in a district with a high special education placement rate for children of color. On the other hand, a campus having 10% less than the district average of Latino students enrolled in Advanced Placement classes would be cause for concern.

In the next section, we provide an extended illustration of how district-level equity auditing can be operationalized from a district with which we have worked in Texas. North East Independent School District (NEISD) in San Antonio, Texas, took up the challenge of equity auditing in a serious and committed way and developed their own approach to addressing the issues it revealed.

DISTRICT EQUITY AUDITS APPLIED: NORTH EAST ISD'S STORY OF THE DEVELOPMENT OF DATA COACHING*

The impact of NCLB's mandate to include students with disabilities in state assessment and accountability systems was soon felt in school systems around the United States. By 2005, when NCLB's provisions were fully phased in, North East Independent School District (NEISD) in San Antonio, Texas, had four campuses initially identified by the state accountability system as low-performing schools based solely on the performance of special education students on state assessments. In this section, we tell our story of how the district bounced back from this serious failure, identified inequities in the system, and then created a process that held all campuses accountable for the achievement of all

Authors' note: This section was written in collaboration with Antoinette F. Riester-Wood, Judith Moening, and Alicia H. Thomas of North East Independent School District.

their students, including students with disabilities, through a close collaboration between central office and campus leaders. We call it the NEISD version of *data coaching* (see also Love, Stiles, Mundry, & DiRanna, 2008).

NEISD Faces a Problem

North East Independent School District is a large, diverse, fast growing, suburban/urban district with a history of excelling in the state accountability system.

The 2004–2005 school year found the district with a record of four schools being initially rated *academically unacceptable* under the Texas accountability system, and ten schools failing to make *adequate yearly progress* (AYP) under the federal system. This large number of failing accountability ratings was a shocking surprise for district and campus leaders as well as for board members, teachers, parents, and community members in a district that historically viewed itself as highly successful. In response, our close review of the data clearly showed that the performance of students in special education was the reason for these poor accountability ratings.

District Leaders Design a Solution

In formulating a solution for the problem of low ratings due to the performance on state assessments by special education students, we used data produced by federal, state, and local accountability systems to identify inequities in the school system. Subsequently, we collectively (and often painfully) examined our core beliefs and then committed to a path of equity and excellence for all students. Along the

Table 7.1 North East ISD Student Demographic Profile 2005–2006	
Total students	59,824
African American	6.9%
Hispanic	44.0%
Limited English proficiency	5.7%
Special education	12.3%
Economically disadvantaged	38.0%

way, we reflected on, revised, and retooled our curricular and instructional practices to create districtwide structures that supported the achievement of all students.

With the full support of the superintendent and the board of trustees, a district leadership team led by the associate superintendent was formed that included professional staff stakeholders from curriculum and instruction, information technology, and special education. We consulted experts and systematically examined and deconstructed our practices to reveal and understand the multiple underpinnings of systemic inequities that resulted in the low performance of special education students. This school systemwide "archeological dig" uncovered severely fragmented programs, poorly understood and complex accountability systems, and lowered standards for students with disabilities. As a result of this work, a new grasp of systemic inequities forced bold decisions that involved risky, uncharted territory for district, campus, and student-achievement goals.

We knew we needed to revise, renew, and retool, and we began by learning about a collaboration between the Harvard Graduate School of Education and the Boston Public Schools (Boudett, Murnane, City, & Moody, 2005). We read about systemic work with campus administrators to teach both the tools and a process for continual school improvement through ongoing review of student data. Based on this model, our district leadership team morphed into a *data coaching team*. The large group reorganized into smaller subteams composed of a general educator, a special educator, and a technology specialist. Each small data coaching team worked with 8–10 campuses throughout the school year focusing on four separate assignments. The purpose of these "Data Coaching Assignments" was to create a partnership between central office and each campus to examine every school in the district and to align beliefs and practices. We believed that it was the responsibility of central office staff to provide leadership, direction, and support to ensure that all campuses aligned instruction for all students, including students with disabilities, in a way that provided the greatest opportunity of success for each and every student.

This districtwide data coaching work was guided by three research-based non-negotiables. The first of these was a set of core beliefs adapted from the work of McKenzie, Skrla, and Scheurich (2006):

1. All children are capable of high levels of academic success.

2. Academic success equitably includes all student groups.

3. Adults in schools are primarily responsible.

4. Traditional school practices result in inequity and must be changed.

Central office and campus leaders throughout the district participated in book studies and professional development sessions during 2004–2006 and focused on the importance of these beliefs (what the authors call "equity consciousness") in creating schools that are both equitable and excellent.

The second non-negotiable was a commitment to rigor and high expectations by providing every special education student access to the general education curriculum to the maximum extent possible. The district had taken steps toward implementation of this non-negotiable during the 2004–2005 school year by reviewing and when necessary, modifying placement and assessment decisions for every child served through special education in NEISD.

The third non-negotiable was a comprehensive program of professional development with an intense focus on the use of research-based instructional strategies in every classroom. Across the district at every campus, teachers used specific strategies, drawing on Marzano and colleagues, for student engagement and focused, immediate feedback to students coupled with goal setting strategies (e.g., Marzano, 2003).

Data Coaching Is Implemented

Feedback to adults was the essence of the NEISD data coaching process. Principals and campus leadership teams received four data coaching assignments from the central office throughout the 2005–2006 school year. "Assignment 1" required principals to review their previous year's campus data and to create a short PowerPoint presentation to share with their faculty on the first day of the new school year. The purposes of the presentations were to summarize the campus data, identify strengths and challenges within the data, and then lay out a plan for addressing those issues.

District-level data coaches met with each principal and his or her leadership team to provide input and assistance prior to delivery of the presentation to campus faculty. For some principals, this was her or his first PowerPoint presentation, and so the data coaching process included tips on the use of that technology tool. In fact, not all principals were successful at their first attempt at creating a presentation that met the requirements set by the district data coaching team and thus had to meet with the central office team multiple times before completing Assignment 1.

By October of the 2005–2006 school year, it was clear that this data coaching process was hard work. Campus leaders had to dig deeper into their data than they ever had before, and they had to review the placement and achievement of every child because every child counted. The second data coaching assignment then required campus teams to put faces to the data by listing students by name using Excel spreadsheets and creating an intervention plan for working with each student at risk of failure. As the district-level data coaches met with principals and their leadership teams to support Assignment 2, we encountered some resistance. Some campuses interpreted this support as interference or criticism of their efforts, but we persevered in helping each campus take a hard look at each individual student's instructional program. The mantra was, "Everybody Counts!"

In January, Assignment 3 required campuses to review all students who were of concern based upon results of district-created benchmark tests. The lists included all special education students. Campus intervention plans were again reviewed and adjusted as part of the "Revise-Renew-Retool" process. By this point in the year, all campuses understood the sense of urgency, and most were on board with the process. Also, this point was an opportunity for midcourse correction, and schools that were not on track for success were required to rework their plan and to return for a second or even a third meeting with their central office data coaches. As a result, the data-coaching message was one of both pressure as well as support. In other words, failure was not an option, but the campuses were not in the struggle alone.

From the results of Assignment 3, we determined that there were campuses still needing additional help, and a new district support structure evolved. Consequently, Schools Needing an Acceleration Program (SNAP) teams were quickly formed for schools needing an accelerated program. Central office staff members formed SNAP teams and fanned out to the district and spent hours weekly on site providing targeted assistance to students and teachers in need of extra help. This support involved central office staff tutoring groups of students, teaching classes so that teachers could run tutoring groups, walking through classrooms with campus administrators to encourage teachers, or anything else which might be of support to students. Our attitude was, "Whatever it takes. We are all in this together." For example, some schools opted to run afterschool-tutoring groups, and the transportation department supported their efforts by running buses as late as 6:30 p.m.

A fourth and final round of data coaching occurred in June. For Assignment 4, campuses were asked to review two years of testing results, describe their significant instructional interventions, and identify those teachers who were clearly content experts. Campus leaders and their leadership teams used those results to draft their campus improvement plans for the upcoming 2006–2007 school year. In addition, these meetings were a celebration of student and campus successes.

The Results

State achievement test results received in May 2006 showed that district data coaching activities supported a dramatic, districtwide improvement in student achievement, especially for students with disabilities. The district tested over 90% of special education students on grade-level standards.

All schools were acceptable or above, and 70% of all schools performed at the level of "Recognized" or "Exemplary," the two top-rating categories under the state system's four categories of ratings. An additional, especially exciting, result was that four of the ten SNAP schools were Recognized.

Table 7.2	Testing Profile for All NEISD Students, 2005–2006		
	Special Education Students Tested on Grade Level (state exam plus the state alternative assessment)	*Special Education Students Passing State Exam*	*General Education Students Passing State Exam*
Reading	91.4%	85%	93.0%
Math	91.3%	71%	82.0%

What We Learned

What did we learn over the course of the year with the data coaching process in NEISD? We learned that the current accountability system is so fast changing and is so complex that campuses can become confused, lose focus, and thus, be at risk of failure unless they receive coherent, focused district support. The ongoing partnership between central office data coaches and campus leadership teams provided a structure for identifying campuses that needed redirection and support without waiting for the summative evaluation provided by state accountability tests toward the end of the school year.

In addition, the combination of support along with pressure from the central office was a key feature of this work. We also learned that this systemic change required a system—a systematic effort was quickly put in place, was communicated as important by the district leadership, was coherent and focused, was data- and research-based, and was persistently worked on all the way through to success. Indeed, what we learned about such systems was much larger than this one area of need. We learned that whenever a district needs a change to equitably serve all students, we always need to set up a system with these characteristics.

The upcoming school year finds our entire district of more than 60 schools committed to the concept of data coaching and its inherent feature of joint planning activities between central office and campus leadership teams. We have come to understand and fully believe that when district and campus leaders collaborate and truly focus their efforts, they can make a difference in the academic success of literally all students, including students served through special education. We have come to understand that creating equitable education requires systemic efforts, like the one we have described here, to change practices.

CHAPTER CONCLUSION

In this chapter, we have described the process for applying equity audits to the school district level. We've made the case for considering campus deviation from the district average or mean as the preliminary step in conducting district-level equity audits. We've suggested a 10% deviation from the district mean as the level that would signal the need for closer examination of a campus data in any particular area. We've also devoted the majority of this chapter to telling the story of a single Texas district, North East ISD, that began with a district-level equity audit and came up with a locally designed, process-oriented solution—called data coaching—to address the issues revealed by the initial audit.

DISCUSSION QUESTIONS AND ACTIVITIES

1. The NEISD leadership team discovered upon making their first data-coaching assignment to campus principals that many of their principals needed substantial assistance from central office staff to appropriately analyze their campuses' data and to put together a presentation on those data. Would the same be true for principals in your district if such an assignment were made? Are sufficient resources available for the principals who need assistance to get it?

2. NEISD decided that participation of students served through special education in appropriate instruction and assessment was their largest challenge. What do you predict would be the biggest issue revealed by an equity audit of your district? How would you begin to make a plan for this need to be addressed?

Part III

Equity Audit Follow-Up Actions and Strategies

8 Becoming an Equity-Oriented Change Agent

Change does not roll in on the wheels of inevitability, but comes through continuous struggle.

—Martin Luther King, Jr.

As we have discussed throughout this book, equity audits are tools that you can use to improve equity within your school or district. These audits will reveal patterns of equity and inequity in three broad areas of the system in place in your schools and districts. However, just knowing that the inequities and equities exist will not automatically lead to a plan for change. In the remainder of this book, we sharpen our focus on the beliefs, attitudes, and actions that are necessary to respond to the challenges for change created by the equity audit. In this chapter specifically, we focus on the leader who will be using the equity audit. In other words, our focus here is on you.

What kind of understanding do you need to have to be able to use these tools with your colleagues? It is not as if all of your fellow teachers, administrators, professional staff, and so forth are just going to immediately and totally embrace equity tools or even equity itself. Indeed, we can virtually promise that you are going to run into multiple kinds and different degrees of resistance.

Some colleagues will just not want to change what they have always done and/or what they have always thought. Other colleagues will hold conscious or unconscious prejudices against children of color, children whose parents have low incomes, children with learning differences, children whose home languages and cultures are different than the mainstream, and so on. Still other colleagues will just not like you or the way you approach change. Thus, it becomes critically important to figure out how to work as a leader with your colleagues in a way that will facilitate change over time.

Being a change agent, an equity agent, or a civil rights worker, as we called this kind of work in our first Corwin book *Leadership for Equity and Excellence*, is not easy. In fact, it is very hard work. What we will do in this chapter, drawing on our own range of experiences as change agents or civil rights workers in schools, districts, and universities, is provide some advice that we hope will help you.

CHARACTERISTICS OF AN EQUITY-ORIENTED CHANGE AGENT (EOCA)

EOCA Has an Equity Attitude

We imagine that you have heard the argument that the "means to an end" or a goal must have the same basic qualities as the "end" you have in mind. In other words, if a school leader wants teachers to be caring and respectful to African American students, that school leader needs to be caring and respectful to teachers. Or if a school leader wants teachers to use more discussion and less direct teaching in the classroom, it would be helpful if the leader used more discussion and less direct talk in teacher meetings. Some would call this modeling (e.g., Bandura & Walters, 1963). You model what you want others to learn and do. Thus, if you want your colleagues to have an equity attitude toward their students, you need to have an equity attitude toward your colleagues.

What does it mean, though, to have an equity attitude toward your colleagues? To us, it means that no matter what your colleagues' personalities are, no matter what their attitudes or assumptions are, no matter what their prejudices and biases are (we will discuss later "courageous" conversations [Singleton & Linton, 2006]), you treat them with respect, appreciation, and care. If in an equity-oriented school, we want to foster all adults treating all children with respect, appreciation, and care, then we must treat all adults the very same way.

If we do not do this, we undermine where we are trying to go—creating an equity-oriented school that serves all children well. Thus, if you do not treat all adults this way, your *means* undermine your *ends*.

Of course, this is easy to say and very hard to do. We all have colleagues who are negative or cynical or who do not seem to care or who just seem to be interested in her or his paycheck or who have hostility or other negative judgments about the school's children or parents or neighborhoods. We all have colleagues we do not think should even be working in our schools. We have colleagues who have short tempers. We have colleagues who will not cooperate or will not carry their fair share of the work. We have colleagues whom we do not trust to be honest with us. We have colleagues who do not think women can be as good as leaders as men or who do not think women know as much as men. We have colleagues who are prejudiced toward their colleagues who are of a different race or ethnicity than they are. We have colleagues we think are emotionally troubled. We have colleagues we believe to be destructive. We have colleagues who are always just trying to feather their nests or serve only themselves. We have colleagues who are caught up in the political games or caught up in pleasing those in authority. For many reasons, we will all have colleagues whom we do not want to work with or are hard to work with.

However, we are strongly recommending that to have an equity attitude and to create a school or district that succeeds equitably with all children, it is necessary to treat *everyone* with respect, appreciation, and care—no exceptions. This does not mean, though, that problems do not get addressed. This does not mean that prejudice, bias, destructiveness, insensitivity, and so forth do not get addressed. In fact, we would argue that addressing difficult issues and having courageous conversations are necessary aspects of treating everyone with respect, appreciation, and care. In fact, we would argue the lack of courageous conversations is disrespectful to others. But addressing difficult issues and having courageous conversations must always be done in interactions that are characterized by respect, appreciation, and care toward everyone.

EOCA Avoids Demonizations

This characteristic is closely connected to the prior one. Demonizations are characterizing someone wholly by one negative characteristic or characterizing someone as totally negative. For example, you have repeatedly seen a colleague treating other colleagues in a negative or hostile way, so you characterize that person solely by these actions. Certainly, if the person is consistently negative or hostile, that person may well be as destructive to others, but a demonization is when you see that person as totally characterized by these actions and do not see other characteristics of the person. In other words, people are very complex; they have many characteristics, usually a combination of some positive and some negative. But when you reduce all of who they are to one negative characteristic and then make that characteristic the essence of who they are or all of who they are, that is demonization.

This is especially a problem when you get angry with someone or when someone does something you find hurtful or insensitive for you. It then becomes worse when someone repeatedly behaves in this same negative way. Eventually, what often happens is that you begin to see this person in terms of one globalized or totalized way—a racist, a sexist, a cynic, dysfunctional, disturbed, and so on.

While it is very seductive and very emotionally satisfying to be able to characterize someone you do not like as wholly a destructive or hurtful person, these judgments or characterizations, these demonizations, are destructive to creating an equity-oriented environment in your school or district. To create an environment that is characterized by the treatment of all children with respect, appreciation, and care, we have to model the treatment of all adults in the very same way.

This "no demonizations" approach, though, does not mean we do not have to have difficult, courageous conversations with our colleagues about the negative ways they are treating students or the negative way they are treating some of their colleagues or the negative ways you perceive they are treating you. It is absolutely necessary to have such conversations even though they are often very difficult, but such difficult conversations will become all but impossible if you are demonizing the person you need to dialogue with.

EOCA Initiates Courageous Conversations

In their book *Courageous Conversations About Race: A Field Guide for Achieving Equity in Schools*, Singleton and Linton (2006) define a "courageous conversation" as one that has the following characteristics:

1. *Engages* those who won't talk.

2. *Sustains* the conversation when it gets uncomfortable or diverted.

3. *Deepens* the conversation to the point where authentic understanding and meaningful actions occur. (p. 16)

In addition, they contend that for educators to engage in courageous conversations, they must commit to four agreements:

1. Stay engaged.

2. Speak your truth.

3. Experience discomfort.

4. Expect and accept nonclosure. (p. 17)

This advice is a good starting point to what we mean by "initiates courageous conversations."

Although Singleton and Linton (2006) are helping educators to have courageous conversations about race, wonderful work on their part and work we all badly need, our focus here is broader than this. We agree that conscious or unconscious, intended or unintended, racism is one of the largest barriers to equitable schools in this country, and we agree that this is one area in which we badly need courageous conversations. Nonetheless, we want to use this concept of courageous conversations to apply to all kinds of difficult conversations we need to have with our colleagues.

Building off of and expanding their definition of a courageous conversation, we want to provide our advice for those wanting to have courageous conversations in their schools:

1. Throughout the conversation, treat everyone with respect, appreciation, and care.

2. Engage with the other person or persons in the fullness of who they are, not just in terms of their problems or the problems you perceive.

3. Stay fairly and openly engaged with everyone in the conversation.

4. Forgive yourself if you fail, become imbalanced, or lose your temper; as soon as you can, return to a fair and open engagement.

5. Be willing to apologize when you make mistakes or treat someone badly.

6. Know that you too have problems and weaknesses and make mistakes and then be willing for those to be part of the conversation; be willing to have others have courageous conversations with you.

7. Do not be afraid to speak your perspective (your truth) while understanding that it is only yours and not necessarily *the truth*.

8. Be willing to experience discomfort and be willing to experience others as discomforted; do not become afraid or uncomfortable with discomfort and thus rush to remove it.

9. Work to include everyone in the conversation to equitably participate in the conversation.

10. Do not fear anger, resentment, fear itself, or distancing; just keep working to have an engaged conversation.

11. Constantly work to move the conversation to deeper, more open levels.

12. Expect and accept that one or many such conversations will not immediately lead to happy endings or even closure.

None of these are easy to do, and they will require a great deal of practice and experience to get better at them. We too are always working on using these and failing and working on them again and again.

In terms of these conversations, the easiest thing in the world is to believe that we have the Truth and that our judgments of others are almost always correct. However, when we fall for this and become seduced by this kind of egotism, we are undermining an equity consciousness, and we are undermining the creation of an environment characterized by equity toward all, which is what is necessary to create equitable educational environments for all children. In other words, one of our largest barriers to having courageous conversations will not be other people; it will be our own egotisms and ourselves.

Clearly, these kinds of conversations are very difficult. There is little wonder that we all tend to avoid them. They are hard work. They require that we remain as balanced and centered as possible in the midst of difficult emotional pressures. They require that we take risks with our own vulnerabilities, fears, and insecurities. They require the danger of being open with others, even others we do not like. They require courage, not just effort, which is why Singleton and Linton (2006) rightly called them "courageous conversations."

EOCA Demonstrates Persistence

To be an equity-oriented change agent, you must be persistent. The inequities in our environments did not arise yesterday. They are not simple, superficial features of our environments. Typically, they are a deep part of the status quo; people are used to them and depend on them; they are often deeply embedded in daily institutional life. In addition, there are many behavior patterns, institutional rules and procedures, habits, and assumptions of mind that, though they are not in and of themselves inequities, support inequities.

For example, "zero tolerance" is to some degree an effort to make educational environments safe for all children and adults (Epp & Watkinson, 1997). Thus, to enact zero tolerance policies, rules and procedures get set up. However, one inequitable result that is occurring all across the country is that these zero tolerance policies are being disproportionately applied to African American boys (Skiba & Noam, 2001). As a result, if equity is our goal, we have to question the policy itself, the rules and procedures designed to implement the policy, and the attitudes and assumptions of those applying those rules and procedures. Some of the aspects of this problem may not be inequitable in and of themselves, but the result or effect may be inequitable.

Thus, to remove embedded inequities of this or any sort requires persistence. For example, changing zero tolerance policies will not be easy. It will not simply be a matter of questioning such policies once or twice, and then everyone will agree to change them. Unless there has been some catastrophic failure of the policy, changing the policy will require persistence. Indeed, for almost any inequity, removing or changing it will require persistent, long-term effort. It will require constant focus, repeated effort, and endurance.

We know from our own experiences that this kind of persistence is difficult. However, as we said at the beginning of this section, inequities are often deeply embedded in ourselves and our institutional environments. Also, getting change of any sort in both people and institutions is hard work that takes time. Persistence, then, is a key characteristic of an equity-oriented change agent.

EOCA Remains Committed but Patient

Standing right next to persistence is patience. Unfortunately, institutions, policies, practices, and people do not change over time or within one week or one month. If you are persistent but impatient, this will be communicated to those around you with the result being more difficult and more resistance. If people feel you are impatient with them, they will experience this as a negative judgment. In addition, if you are impatient, you will wear yourself out, and being an equity agent is long-term work, so maintaining over the long term is necessary.

However, when we counsel patience, we are not saying to let changes go too slowly. You can become so patient that you are pushing change at a slow pace. In fact, the tipping point between not patient enough and too patient is a tough one to know. If you try to go too fast, you will undermine all that you are doing; if you try to go too slow, you will undermine all that you are doing. And unfortunately, no yellow flag will suddenly appear to tell you which side of the tipping point you are on.

Judging this point is just flat out hard. Some of your best friends and allies will tell you that you are impatient and trying to move too fast. At the same time, some of your best friends and allies will tell you that you are being too patient and not moving fast enough. Any change agent is always caught between these two, and the line is messy and ambiguous.

The only remedy to this dilemma that we know is to pay attention. If you are trying to push change too fast, many people will resist or complain or say something to you about this. If you are trying to change too slowly, few to none will resist or complain except for those who want the same change you want. The fact is that sometimes you will go too fast, and sometimes you will go too slowly. Just pay attention and try to learn from your experience; this is maybe not the best advice, but it is the best advice we have.

One of the hardest parts of doing equity work is maintaining commitment and patience. You know inequity hurts your students. You know inequity hurts all of us. Yet you cannot successfully facilitate the creation of more equitable environments without patience toward others and patience toward yourself. To be successful, you have to be in this for the long haul, and the long haul requires patience.

EOCA Maintains an Assets Attitude

One of the first people to model for us what we mean by an assets attitude was Dr. Miguel Guajardo, who works with the Llano Grande Center for Research and Development, a community activist center in the Rio Grande Valley of Texas. One of Llano Grande's fundamental assumptions is that in doing community organizing, you start with a focus on the community's assets. Another source of our learning on this has been the work of Dr. Luis Moll and his colleagues (1992, 2005). Moll and his colleagues focus on what they call "the funds of knowledge" that Latino/a students bring with them to school from their families, neighborhoods, and culture. In both of these cases, there is a primary focus on assets rather than on deficits.

We have taken this focus and reframed it as a characteristic of equity workers. If you are going to work on changing a classroom, a school, or a district, it is best to start with the assets that are already in place. And every place and every person has assets, which can be identified. Once you know what these are, you need to constantly build on them as your foundations or starting points for change.

For example, let's say that the academic performance of your school is inadequate. However, the school has a history of strong support from the community. To use an assets orientation, you would ask how you could build from this history of community support to improve the academic performance of the students. You might bring the community in and involve them in developing ways to improve academic performance. You might develop student-parent contracts on student homework. You might recruit parents to run a Saturday academic academy. There are easily hundreds of different ideas, but the main point is to start with your assets and build them up.

This same approach can be used in working with individuals. Every individual has assets of one sort or another. Since we all want to be valued, validating a person's assets is critically important to building a positive relationship with a person. We are not talking manipulation here; we are talking values. We believe that an equity orientation *requires* a valuing of all people no matter who they are. This does not mean that you should not have courageous conversations with someone over difficulties or, say, the mistreatment of children. You do have to have those conversations, but our point is that one key aspect of any conversation and any positive relationship is the recognition and valuing of the person's assets. Then, if you can start with valuing a person's assets, you will have a good foundation to move forward with change or with courageous conversations.

You also need to value your own assets. If you are like us, we are always getting down on ourselves for our mistakes, which we make frequently. As equity work requires long-term endurance, you have to maintain some reserve of valuing your own assets. We are not talking, though, of feeding our egos. Instead, we are talking about a balanced, persistent awareness that we, too, have assets that need to be valued.

EOCA Maintains a Coherent Focus

To move people and/or an organization toward more equity requires maintaining a coherent focus. Sonny Donaldson, former superintendent of the Aldine, Texas, school district (a district that has made great progress in closing achievement gaps and raising student performance for all its students) always said to us when we were doing research in his district that "the main thing is to keep the main thing the main thing." While we know this particular saying has been used and said by many others, Sonny Donaldson meant persistently maintaining a coherent focus on improving instruction in his district over time.

This consistent and persistent focus through time is critical to improving equity in your school or district. Indeed, as we have said, creating any kind of sustainable change is very difficult. Change that moves your school or district toward greater equity is truly long, hard work. Thus, to be successful, you will need to maintain your focus over time. In other words, you cannot keep switching areas of focus each week or month. Instead, you need to keep reminding yourself what your focus is and keep communicating that focus. For example, many of the most successful leaders say they say the same thing over and over as they successfully facilitate change in an organization.

CHAPTER CONCLUSION

We fully understand that understanding and using the seven characteristics of an equity-oriented change agent that we have discussed will be very difficult. We know from our own weekly efforts to maintain these characteristics that we often fail. We sometimes want to demonize someone. We, too, want to avoid courageous conversations. We forget to emphasize an assets orientation. You cannot fail any more frequently than we do.

Thus, a mistake we can all make is to torture ourselves over these failures. Certainly, it is important to recognize our failures and learn from them, and it is not helpful to assume or think we do not all fail constantly in our efforts to lead with an equity attitude. On the other hand, it is an unproductive energy drain to constantly torture ourselves over these failures.

This is yet another place in which finding balance is important. We need to recognize our mistakes, reflect upon them so that we learn, and then move on. This equity work is difficult, but it is also a call to our hearts and minds, a call to make a substantial difference in the lives of *all* of our children. It is, as we have previously said, the civil rights work of our day, and we hope this discussion of the characteristics needed to be an equity-oriented change agent will help you accomplish that work.

DISCUSSION QUESTIONS AND ACTIVITIES

1. Many of the schools and districts with whom we have worked have had success with book studies in which leadership teams from campuses and/or the district participate over the course of a semester or year. An obvious choice for a book study related to this chapter would be Singleton and Linton's (2006) *Courageous Conversations*.

2. Visit the Web site of the Llando Grande Center, http://www.llano grande.org, to learn about their assets-oriented approach to schooling.

3. Which of the characteristics of an equity-oriented change agent do you think you possess in the greatest depth? Which will be growth areas for you? How would you answer the same questions about the other members of your leadership team? How do you think they would answer them about themselves? About you?

9 Increasing Equity Consciousness

At the risk of sounding ridiculous, let me say that the true revolutionary is guided by feelings of love.

—Ernesto (Che) Guevara

In the previous chapter, we discussed the importance and characteristics of being an equity-oriented change agent. The change to which we are referring begins with a school in which some students or student groups may be learning at high levels, but where not all students or student groups are learning at these levels. In other words, there are inequities in student performance, and these inequities are represented by the "achievement gap." Since there is an achievement gap among student groups in nearly all schools, all districts, all states, and thus, a nationwide gap in achievement, we can surmise that what we have been doing in the past and what we are currently doing in schools is not working or at least not working in most schools, districts, and states. So then, change is needed if we indeed are working to create schools that are excellent and equitable. But what exactly are we trying to change and where do we get started?

Changing schools is complex, and as fervently as we seek to do it, we have yet to find the "silver bullet" of reform that works in all schools, and we probably never will. One thing that research consistently has found, however, is that teacher quality matters. Although there is debate as to what constitutes teacher quality (e.g., Darling-Hammond, 2000, 2001; McCaffrey, Lockwood, Koretz, & Hamilton, 2003) and what the relationship is between teacher quality and student achievement (e.g., Heck, 2007), we know students achieve more in some teachers' classrooms than in others (Rivkin, Hanushek, & Kain, 2001; Rowan, Correnti, & Miller, 2002), and presumably, a significant factor is these students' success is the quality of the teaching. Thus, returning to our question as to where the equity-oriented change agent should begin, we contend the starting point should be improving teacher quality.

The two aspects of teacher quality we describe in this chapter and the next are teacher-equity consciousness and teacher instructional skills. If indeed in every classroom in a school there was a teacher with a well-developed equity consciousness and well-developed teaching skills, we believe the achievement gap in that school would be eliminated. Going further, if in every school in a system there were teachers in every classroom with well-developed equity consciousness and well-developed teaching skills, the gap would be eliminated within that school system. So, you get the picture: if in every classroom, if in every school, if in every system there was high quality teaching by an equity-conscious teacher, the nationwide achievement gap would be eliminated.

Having been school teachers and administrators, we do understand that this is not as easily accomplished as it is stated here. But it can be done. Indeed, from our own work studying high performing school districts, there are examples of districts in which it has been done (Skrla & Scheurich, 2001; Skrla, Scheurich, & Johnson, 2000). Hopefully, this chapter, as well as the others devoted to "strategies" for transforming schools into ones that are equitable and excellent, will give you some tools on which to draw. We will begin in this chapter with a discussion of equity consciousness, follow in Chapter 10 with a consideration of equity-oriented teaching skills, and conclude this strategies section in Chapter 11 with suggestions for avoiding equity traps and developing equity skills.

DEFINING EQUITY CONSCIOUSNESS

By equity consciousness we mean that teachers are aware of, accept, and act on four central beliefs:

1. That all children (except only a very small percentage, e.g., those with profound disabilities) are capable of high levels of academic success.

2. That *all* children means *all*, regardless of a child's race, social class, gender, sexual orientation, learning differences, culture, language, religion, and so on.

3. That the adults in schools are primarily responsible for student learning.

4. That traditional school practices may work for some students but are not working for *all* children. Therefore, if we are going to eliminate the achievement gap, it requires a change in our practices.

In the past, researchers, professors, and leadership practitioners have described teachers as either having an equity consciousness (as defined above) or not having an equity consciousness. That is, a teacher either "got it" or "didn't get it." However, teachers' attitudes and beliefs are much more complex than either having or not having an equity consciousness. It is not an all or nothing situation, and it is usually not a conscious decision to think or believe a certain way. It is just not that simple. Teachers, like all people, are complex.

A CONTINUUM OF EQUITY CONSCIOUSNESS

For example, some teachers may have almost no equity consciousness for a variety of reasons. Some, perhaps, have never been exposed to the concept, having never even considered that what they do in their classrooms could be producing inequities. Others may uncritically accept their own deficit thinking (Valencia, 1997). That is, teachers may blame parents for students' lack of learning—"These parents just don't value education." They may assume low-income status means a limited ability to learn—"These children just don't come to school with any experiences." They may attribute a lack of student success to factors external to themselves and the school—"It's not us; it's these children and their families" (McKenzie, 2001). Still other teachers may hold deeply rooted (but most often unspoken) prejudicial views toward the students they teach, including a belief in the genetic inferiority of some student groups (Chellman, Weinstein, Stiefel, & Schwartz, 2005; Lyman & Villani, 2004).

A second group of teachers may have a limited equity consciousness. These teachers may have some understanding of equity issues for one specific group of students but may fail to make connections to other groups experiencing similar discrimination. For example, a

teacher may teach special education classes and have a strong awareness of how students with learning differences experience marginalization in schools, but this teacher may not see that the same systemic
marginalization happens to students of color, to English language
learners, to students from low-income families, and to other groups.

A third possible group may be teachers who appear to have developed an equity consciousness, who can even articulate it but whose
behavior does not match what they say they believe. We call this
an inauthentic equity consciousness. Often, these teachers see themselves as having altruistic motives—working in low-income schools to
serve as role models or to "save" the children (McKenzie, 2001).
Unfortunately, this type of inauthentic equity consciousness may have
more to do with the teacher's own esteem needs than it does with actually serving all students well.

Still another possibility in the range of teachers' equity consciousness is the group that seems to have an equity consciousness and
shows indications of deeply understanding it but tends to slip back into
one of the groups already discussed herein, especially when frustrated
or under stress. This, then, is a vacillating equity consciousness.
Sometimes this vacillation comes when teachers present the only or
minority voice in support of students, their families, and community
and face the silencing and norming efforts of others who seem unwill-
ing to let go of their own deficit views and attempt to impose these
views on everyone else (McKenzie & Scheurich, 2004).

The final category of equity consciousness is the group of teachers who have it, understand it, and live it out on a daily basis. This we
call an authentic equity consciousness. Teachers, when asked how they
developed this consciousness, cite their difficult childhood circumstances, connections between their equity beliefs and their religious
faith or spirituality (Dantley, 2003), the influence of a mentor or
teacher who had a well-developed equity consciousness, or a critical
incident that changed forever their views of those unlike themselves.

Consequently, since teachers are on a continuum in regard to their
equity consciousness—with some having little equity consciousness,
some having well-developed equity consciousness, and others falling
somewhere in between—an equity-oriented change agent needs to
understand that to help all teachers improve requires different instructional leadership approaches for different teachers. Principals, tradition-
ally, even when they understand the importance of cultivating an equity

consciousness among their faculty, have provided only one type of professional development for everyone. For example, the entire faculty may participate in a book study about successful teachers of diverse students. Most likely though, all the teachers on a faculty will not benefit equally or will not benefit at all from such an activity. This is because different teachers are at different levels in their equity-consciousness development, and a meaningful professional development activity for some teachers will, therefore, not be a meaningful professional activity for other teachers. Principals, thus, should provide differentiated professional development for individual teachers or small groups of teachers with similar equity consciousness needs, just as teachers in classrooms should provide differentiated instruction for individual students or small groups of students with similar needs. To assist principals in this task, we provide the following research-based strategies that can be employed in a customized and individualized way to help teachers grow and develop their equity consciousness (Goddard, Hoy, & Woolfolk, 2000; Mezirow, 2000; Taylor, Marienau, & Fiddler, 2000).

INSTRUCTIONAL LEADERSHIP STRATEGIES TO DEVELOP TEACHERS' EQUITY CONSCIOUSNESS

1. Use equity-focused professional development materials such as the following:
   - Guided book studies
   - Films
   - Interactive media
   - Commercial curricula

2. Promote reflection of and learning from critical incidents through the use of the following:
   - Journals
   - Accountability data analysis
   - Videotaped lessons
   - Peer observations
   - Critical friends groups

3. Use social persuasion consisting of the following:
   - Constant repetition of the equity message
   - Guest speakers who reinforce the message

- Reframing deficit comments regarding students, their families, and community into acknowledgments of assets

4. Prescribe actions and behaviors to increase understanding of students' cultures and homes:
   - Positive phone calls to students' homes
   - Home visits
   - Neighborhood walks

5. Model respectful and culturally responsive interactions:
   - Caring principal-teacher relationships
   - Principal modeling respect and cultural responsiveness
   - Skilled mentor-teacher modeling respect and cultural responsiveness

6. Directly address negative attitudes and low expectations:
   - Deficit thinking
   - Inconsistent logic about students' potential based on faulty assumptions
   - Stereotypes
   - Blaming the students, their families, or culture for the students' lack of success

7. Incrementally raise expectations for students and teachers as positive change occurs.

CHAPTER CONCLUSION

Hopefully, this list offers equity-oriented change agents a toolkit for beginning or continuing their work in helping teachers and themselves develop equity consciousness. Needless to say, however, equity consciousness, though essential, will not be sufficient to transform a school into one that serves all students well. To ensure the success of all students, the leadership must also take into consideration teaching skills, a discussion to which we turn in the following chapter.

DISCUSSION QUESTIONS AND ACTIVITIES

1. If you were to construct a map of where all the staff members in your building were with respect to your estimation of their

current state of equity consciousness, what would it look like? Where would you be on the map?

2. Who is the person in your building who would be the first person you would turn to in seeking an ally to assist in the work of making a plan to systematically raise equity consciousness in your school or school district?

3. Which of the instructional leadership strategies we listed that can help promote increased equity consciousness do you already use? How can these be more carefully and coherently targeted on your campus to promote higher levels of equity consciousness?

10 Developing High- Quality Teaching Skills

Teachers will not come to the school knowing all they have to know, but knowing how to figure out what they need to know, where to get it, and how to help others make meaning out of it.

—*A Nation Prepared*

In the previous chapter, we discussed one of the two essential characteristics a high-quality teacher possesses: equity consciousness. Moreover, we offered strategies an equity-oriented leader can employ to assist teachers in developing equity consciousness. In this chapter, we turn to the next essential characteristic of a high-quality teacher: well-developed teaching skills. First, we will describe these skills and then again offer practical strategies for leaders to use in helping teachers develop or refine their teaching skills.

Although there is a range of opinion regarding the characteristics and teaching skills of high-quality teachers (Berliner, 2001), there are a set of generally agreed upon teaching skills that high-quality teachers employ (e.g., Resnick & Hall, 2001; Saphier, Haley-Speca, & Gower, 2008). It is also assumed, based of the commonalities of teacher-performance assessments among the various states, that the employment of these skills can be observed and evaluated. However, if one is an equity-oriented leader, one must not only be concerned about ensuring that every teacher has these skills but also that every teacher has these skills *and* uses them every day to ensure the success of *every* child.

To help in this effort, we offer here, as well as in previous work, "Preparing Instructional Leaders for Social Justice" (McKenzie, Skrla, & Scheurich, 2006), the following generally accepted teaching skills necessary for high-quality teaching. Accompanying each teaching skill is an evidence statement to help leaders know what to look for when assessing the level of each teaching skill. Following this is a sample professional development strategy, Teaching and Learning Tours, that leaders can use in helping teachers develop these teaching skills.

HIGH-QUALITY TEACHING SKILLS AND EVIDENCE TO ASSESS THEM

Skill 1. Using Consistent and Reliable Classroom Procedures and Routines

Evidence: Students know "how things work here." There is no confusion as to what is to be done, how it is to be done, when it is to done, and so on. Students know the expectations for formatting assignments; they know how to get the teacher's attention; they know when and where to obtain needed materials, supplies, and so forth (Wong & Wong, 2004). Moreover, the routines and procedures are equitably applied. For example, if the teacher establishes the expectation that students are to raise their hands to respond to a question or to get the teacher's attention, all students will be required to do so. In other words, teachers won't hold some students to one standard, that of waiting to be called on prior to speaking, while allowing other students to call out.

Skill 2. Clearly Communicating Expectations for Learning

Evidence: This is similar to consistently using routines and procedures but refers particularly to the learning task. Evidence for this skill can be garnered by asking students what, specifically, they are working on in regard to the assigned task, what they should know or be able to do once they have completed the assignment, why they need to know this information or be able to do or have this particular skill, and how they will judge whether they have done a good job on this assignment (Resnick & Hall, 2001). Typically, some students can answer all these questions. Equity, however, is achieved when all students can answer all these questions.

Skill 3. Stimulating Students With High-Level and Complex Tasks

Evidence: In looking for evidence for this skill, one must be able to discriminate between stimulated and stymied. *Stimulated* would mean that although students may be experiencing cognitive dissonance (Festinger, 1957), they are progressing toward success. Students would experience enough success to stay motivated to continue to engage in the learning task. *Stymied*, however, would mean that students are experiencing enough cognitive dissonance or maybe even confusion that they are frustrated to a level where they cannot imagine success and thus will abandon the task. The best way we know to discern whether a student is stimulated or stymied is to look at the progress the student is making toward the end result and to talk to the student regarding her or his *experience* of the learning. Equity regarding this third skill would require the teacher to know how each student learns, to know how much progress each student is making toward the end result, to recognize when a student is stimulated and when a student is stymied, and to know how to move each and all students to success (e.g., Bell, 2003).

Skill 4. Ensuring Students Are Actively, Cognitively Engaged

Evidence: Students are actively, cognitively engaged if they are thinking, in other words cogitating, about the learning objective. This may sound simplistic, but it is not. We can often be fooled about the level of active cognitive engagement in our classes. For example, we may believe that a student who is looking at the teacher, exhibiting compliant behavior, and possibly nodding is considering the learning objective, making connections, in other words, learning. However, we can give testament from our own experiences when we were students that this may not be the case. Students can appear to be learning when indeed they are thinking of many things other than the learning objective. Therefore, for this skill, teachers need to structure learning so that they monitor students' active cognitive engagement.

For example, in a first-grade classroom, if the learning objective is that students will add single digit numbers, the teacher could provide each student with a small dry erase board. Then, the teacher would ask the students to individually work the problem on their erase boards. Once all students have answered the problem, the teacher would have the students hold up their boards and show their answers to the teacher. Hopefully, this would be done in small groups and differentiated to the needs of the particular students within this group (Tomlinson, 1999; Tomlinson et al., 2003). Using the dry erase boards, the teacher would know exactly which students understood the concept of single digit addition and which did not. This would allow the teacher to make decisions about the next step in the learning process. For example, the teaching might discover that three of the students in the class are continually answering the problems incorrectly. These students would need more guidance, what Hunter (1994) calls "guided practice."

Providing this immediate guidance that is more guided practice based on the assessed needs of each student allows the teacher to attend to any fissure, any little crack, before it becomes a gap. However, what usually occurs is a teacher will ask a group of students a question and then call on one student to answer. This pattern is continued until the teacher is convinced she or he has *taught* the objective. However, often times there are students who do not understand and whose lack of understanding goes unnoticed.

Catching a misunderstanding or a lack of understanding early can prevent a gap and ensure equity (e.g., Yair, 2000).

Skill 5. Extending Student Learning Through Teacher-to-Student and Student-to-Student Discussion

Evidence: Many of us are interactive learners. We don't know what we think about something until we hear ourselves discuss or explain it. In schools, providing opportunities for students to talk aloud to someone can help them understand their thinking. However, it is through asking probing questions in an effort not only to clarify thinking but also to extend thinking that learning goes to a deeper level. Whereas teachers have been trained to use questioning strategies to extend learning, students also need to be explicitly taught to ask questions that extend their learning and the learning of others (e.g., Williamson, Bondy, Langley, & Mayne, 2005). In teaching both teachers and students to ask probing questions and extend learning, we have classrooms full of several teachers rather than merely one. Therefore, equity can be achieved when each student becomes a question answerer and a question poser.

Skill 6. Frequently Assessing Individual Student Learning

Evidence: At the end of each learning segment, lesson, or unit, the teacher uses an assessment, which is most often teacher made, that provides data the teacher can use to determine which students have or have not mastered the objective being taught. Thus, the teacher can determine which students need more instructional guidance. These assessments can be "quick checks," as one school in which we work titles them. Returning to our elementary school example, a quick check for addition might involve students working three or four addition problems on a dry erase board and then showing these to the teacher. The teacher would be able to quickly assess who needs more guided practice in addition. A quick check in high school might include using exit notes. During the last few minutes of class, the teacher can have students write a three or four sentence explanation of what they learned that day related to the lesson objective.

Of course, for these notes to be useful and to promote equity, the teacher would need to read the exit notes that day and then make instructional decisions based on the data revealed through the use of these exit notes. Thus, the teacher might discover that the majority of the students did not take away from the lesson what the teacher intended. The instructional decision, then, might be to change the way the lesson was taught and reteach it to the entire class. The data might reveal that most of the students learned what was intended, but there were a few students that needed to be retaught or needed more guided practice. Equity, however, is only achieved if the teacher uses the data from the quick check to make instructional decisions that are carried out as soon as possible. Waiting several days or a week to reteach or provide more guided practice can create a gap in some students' learning. Moreover, a small gap in first grade can become the Grand Canyon by high school.

Skill 7. Differentiating Instruction to Meet Individual Student Needs and Capitalize on Individual Assets

Evidence: Teachers are using the data from assessments, including quick checks, to make instructional decisions regarding the way they need to differentiate instruction to build on students' assets and ensure that all students are learning at high levels. Differentiation is often discussed as meeting the needs of the gifted and talented or high achieving student or meeting the needs of the student who is below grade level or deemed to need remediation. This results in gifted and talented or advanced placement classes on the one end and foundational classes or tutorials on the other end. Our emphasis here, though, is on differentiating within the school day and within the regular class.

To build on each student's assets, teachers should, as we've already described, assess students often. They should know at the end of each class period or each learning segment which students know and do not know what was being taught and then make instructional decisions at that juncture. Often, though, teachers teach a lesson, sample a few students to see if they understood what was taught, assume all students understood, and then move too quickly for some students into independent practice. Some students just need more guidance. Therefore, to ensure that all students understood what was taught and that all students were ready to move into practicing their new skill, the teacher must assess each student's knowledge prior to moving into independent practice. If the teacher discovers that some students indeed need more guided practice, this guidance needs to occur right away. If the teacher waits until the end of a teaching unit or the end of the week to assess whether students understood a skill or concept and then to provide more guided practice, it is too late for several reasons.

Let's take a simple elementary math concept as an example, although the need for guided practice is just as important in secondary education as it is in elementary. If a second-grade student was learning about regrouping in math, first the student would need to understand the concept of place value. A student cannot understand that 10 ones can be put together to make one 10 if the student does not know there are concepts like "ones" and "tens." Thus, if a teacher assumes students understand place value and then moves along into regrouping, those students who do not know place value will be lost. If the teacher, then, does not assess throughout the lessons on regrouping and waits until the end of the unit or the end of the week to assess, a gap in learning is created. However, if a teacher assesses at the end of each learning segment, the teacher will know which students understand the concepts being taught and which do not.

It is at that time, and not later, that the teacher needs to differentiate the instruction and provide these students with more guided practice—guidance being provided by the teacher who has the skill to move a student to the next level of learning. Typically, skill introduction is not the time to rely on peer teaching. Furthermore, when assessment occurs too long after the initial teaching, student confusion or lack of understanding will not be discovered early enough. This lack of initial learning will prevent the student from learning all the other concepts that depend on this initial skill or concept—a gap occurs. Then, once this gap has begun, the teacher has to try to carve out time in the day or after school to reteach the student. However, if the student had received timely guided instruction, this gap can be prevented. Moreover, if a teacher assesses prior to a lesson being taught and discovers which students have or do not have the requisite skills needed to learn the new concept, the teacher can "preteach" the new concept in a guided small group.

This preteach would focus not only on the needed requisite skill but also introduce the new skill as well. This way, when the teacher introduces the new skill or concept to the entire class, the students who have been pretaught would not be behind; in fact, they will be ahead. This should increase students' confidence in their ability to learn the new concept because they already have been introduced to it. Equity in this skill, then, is providing more guidance for those students who need it at the time they need it, thus, preventing a gap from starting (e.g., Gregory, 2003).

Skill 8. Using an Asset Model to Respond to Students' Varying Cultures

Evidence: A teacher using an asset model in response to the varying cultures of students is "cross-culturally competent, skilled in effectively promoting the social development of culturally diverse learners, and is using the learner's culture as a vehicle for cognitive and social learnings" (Cartledge, Tillman, & Talbert-Johnson, 2001, p. 34). Thus, equity is demonstrated through this skill because the teacher sees all students as competent learners who bring assets from their culture to the learning environment. Asset thinking, unlike deficit thinking (Valencia, 1997) presumes competence. Using asset thinking, a teacher believes students can and will learn, thereby reinforcing in students their beliefs that they are capable learners (e.g., Gay, 2000; Gonzalez & Huerta-Macias, 1997; Ladson-Billings, 1995, 1997). In other words, no student is outside the teacher's zone of self-efficacy (McKenzie & Lozano, 2008).

Skill 9. Demonstrating Respect and Care in All Interactions With All Students and Students' Families

Evidence: Teachers who respect students and students' families demonstrate this respect daily in their words, their tone of voice, and their giving of time and positive attention. Literally, respect is demonstrated in everything a teacher does or does not do, in everything a teacher does or does not put value on. Teachers who respect students and their students' families understand that the ways in which the teacher sees the world may not be the only way in which the world can be seen. This difference in worldview is respected rather than denounced. It is seen as an asset not a deficit. The teacher who truly respects students and their families opens himself or herself up to learning from and with students and their families. This is a difference in attitude from molding students and their families to fit into the teacher's ways of seeing and doing to working alongside students and their families to use the assets each student brings to the classroom to enhance the collective classroom learning.

A STRATEGY FOR DEVELOPING HIGH-QUALITY TEACHING SKILLS: TEACHING AND LEARNING TOURS

There is an array of strategies to assist teachers in developing high-quality teaching skills. Here we focus on one strategy we have used and found to be highly effective—teaching and learning tours.

Teaching and learning tours is a strategy that provides teachers an opportunity for reflecting on their practice. It is in-situ professional development that occurs within the workday and on the school site. We have learned from adult-education theory that for professional learning to be meaningful for adults, it must draw from and apply to their work experiences (Mezirow, 2000). Therefore, in keeping with adult-learning theory, this strategy uses the teachers' working context—their schools, specifically addresses the current challenges students are having, and draws from the teachers' expertise to provide solutions to these challenges.

Thus, the purpose of teaching and learning tours is to provide teachers training focused on one of the previously discussed instructional skill, for example—active cognitive engagement. This is done by taking a small group of teachers on a teaching and learning tour in which they go into a colleague's classroom to observe the skill in practice. However, this is not about teachers evaluating other teacher's classroom practice. It is about using colleagues' classrooms as laboratories for teachers to engage in their own reflective practice. In other words, creating a space where teachers can stand back and see the classroom as a whole—observing the forest from outside the trees.

BOX 10.1

Teaching and Learning Protocol

Focus: Active Cognitive Engagement

- Reminder: This is *not* about the person being observed. It *is* about using your colleague's classroom as a lab for you to engage in *reflective practice*, which is thinking about your practice.
- If this were your classroom, what would you be proud of? What is positive in this classroom?
- What is the objective being taught? Based on this objective, what is the percentage of children who are actively cognitively engaged?
- If this were your classroom, what could you do to "ratchet up" the active cognitive engagement? What other things might you consider to make this lesson or classroom environment even better?
- What have you taken away from this that you will try out in your classroom?

To clarify, we offer below the steps we use in conducting teaching and learning tours.

1. The first time teachers go on "a tour," an explanation is given for the purpose of the tour, emphasizing that this is a professional development activity for reflective practice not teacher evaluation.

2. Teachers meet for about fifteen minutes to review the focus skill and determine what the skill looks like in actual practice.

3. The teaching and learning tour protocol is reviewed (Box 10.1).

4. Teachers go into a classroom for five or ten minutes looking for evidence of the focus skill.

5. After five or ten minutes, teachers leave the classroom and debrief in the hallway using the questions on the protocol.

6. After touring three or four classrooms, a debriefing of the entire tour is conducted.

7. A different set of teachers cycle through these tours during the day. Typically, twenty teachers can participate per day.

8. At the end of the day, a whole school debriefing is conducted, and a combined list of strategies is compiled to address the focus skill—in this example active cognitive engagement (Box 10.2 contains a list recently generated by one school). It is important to note here that the list is generated from the teachers, thereby using their expertise, and is simple enough that teachers can employ the strategies immediately with no need for elaborate planning or preparation. We believe this is consistent with adult-learning theory, focusing on the teachers' immediate challenges and using their expertise to come up with solutions.

BOX 10.2

Strategies Generated From Teaching and Learning Tours

- Teacher-guided small groups instead of teacher moving from individual student to individual student
- Use of white boards for student responses
- Use of timer to move students through transitions and guide individual, small-group, and whole-class responses
- Assign cooperative jobs for small groups
- Use instruction cards for centers
- Utilize coteachers for guiding groups
- Individual student response cards (for example A, B, C, D or yes/no or agree/disagree)
- Use butcher paper in corners of room and have students respond on the paper
- Use butcher paper on the floor and have students respond on the paper
- Use sponge activities when waiting to maximize learning time
- Games that require individual response, then small group, then whole class

- Wait time
- Think, pair, share
- Flexible grouping by student need
- Preteach
- Use of timer or watch for teacher to check active cognitive engagement

The feedback from teachers we have worked with using these tours has been positive. Teachers tell us that observing other teachers' classrooms allowed them to see the big picture. In addition, they say debriefing with other teachers helped them to clarify their thinking and provided them with strategies they could go back and try in their classroom immediately. Indeed, we've taken teachers on a tour in the morning and then visited their classrooms in the afternoon and seen teachers already using the strategies they and their colleagues came up with earlier in the day.

Certainly, this strategy has been useful in assisting individual teachers in developing reflective practice, but it has also assisted schools in developing a community of reflective practitioners who openly share their classrooms with others, thus creating transparency and who engage in professional conversations that move everyone's work forward. We must offer a caution here, however; for this strategy to be effective, the tours must be lead by someone who has the instructional expertise to initially guide the discussion. Having a principal or instructional supervisor attend the tours or guide the tours sends a powerful message as to the value of this type of tour, the value of teachers' time, the value of teachers' expertise in solving problems, and the value of professional development and specifically, reflective practice. Moreover, for this strategy to bring about whole-school reform, to create a schoolwide learning community, these tours will need to become "what we do here." That is, they need to be scheduled throughout the year and consistently done; in other words, they need to be protected from the micro-diversions that take us away from being consistent with reform.

CHAPTER CONCLUSION

In the last two chapters we provided a discussion of the two essential characteristics high-quality teachers possess—an equity consciousness and well-developed teaching skills. In Chapter 9, we described equity consciousness and offered practical strategies leaders can use to help teachers and themselves further develop their equity consciousness. In this chapter, we provided a list of nine teaching skills a high-quality teacher would need to possess and use to be effective with students. Moreover, we offered evidence of what these skills would look like in practice, specifically practice that aims to ensure equity. In the next chapter, we describe the possible traps to equity, defined as "Equity Traps" (McKenzie & Scheurich, 2004) and offer strategies that have proven successful in avoiding these traps and thus improving achievement and programmatic and teacher-quality equity.

DISCUSSION QUESTIONS AND ACTIVITIES

1. We have provided a list of nine skills that high-quality teachers have and know how to use. Do you agree with all nine skills on our list? Which ones would you leave off? What other skills do you think are essential for high-quality teachers to have and use that we have left off our list? Can you point to research that supports your view?

2. What would be necessary at your campus to gain approval for implementing teaching and learning tours? Where would you start? Who could you count on to help you get the idea going?

11 Avoiding Equity Traps and Developing Equity Skills

The path of least resistance and least trouble is a mental rut already made. It requires troublesome work to undertake the alternation of old beliefs.

—John Dewey

This chapter explores the traps that prevent educators from being successful with all students. We call these "equity traps" and define them as

> patterns of thinking and behaviors that trap the possibilities for creating equitable schools for children of color. In other words, they trap equity; they stop or hinder our ability to move toward equity in schooling. Furthermore, these traps are both individual and collective, often reinforced among administrators and

teachers through formal and informal communication, assumptions, and beliefs. (McKenzie & Scheurich, 2004, p. 603)

However, the individual and the collective school staff do not have to fall into these traps. There are equity skills that can be developed that either prevent one from falling into these equity traps or release one from these traps if indeed one falls into them. There are, moreover, strategies for avoiding these traps and developing equity skills. These strategies, along with the equity traps and conversely the equity skills, will be discussed in this chapter. We begin with a discussion of the study that led us to identify equity traps. We then describe each equity trap, the equity skills that prevent or release one from each trap, and the strategies for developing these equity skills.

THE ORIGINAL EQUITY TRAPS STUDY

Equity traps were drawn from a study that one of the authors of this book (McKenzie, 2001) conducted for her dissertation research. At the time of the study, she was a principal of an urban elementary school serving predominantly students of color and those whose families had low or nearly no income. The teaching faculty at the school was predominantly white and female. Although there were some teachers who were highly successful teaching all their students, there were many who were not. Moreover, some of the teachers seemed to believe that they could not teach "these kids," referring to their students of color and those living in low- or no-income homes. Knowing that her school was similar to most urban schools in the United States—that is, most teachers are white, middle class females teaching students of color and those whose family incomes are below middle class— McKenzie wanted to understand why white teachers were having difficulty teaching all their students. Specifically, she wanted to understand the perceptions of white teachers regarding their students of color and themselves as white educators.

In an attempt to understand these perceptions, she conducted a six-month-long qualitative study with six experienced, white teachers at a school that was similar in student population to the school where McKenzie was principal. The results of this research produced findings that were framed as four equity traps: (1) A Deficit View,

(2) Racial Erasure, (3) Avoiding and Employing the Gaze, and (4) Paralogical Beliefs and Behaviors. Subsequently, four skills were conceptualized to prevent individuals and entire school staffs from falling into equity traps. These four traps (and their matching skills) are explored in great detail in the next sections of this chapter. However, the terminology used to label them has evolved somewhat since the original research project. Therefore, we've reframed them to make them more useable for practitioners interested in strategies to address issues uncovered by equity audits.

EQUITY TRAP 1: SEEING ONLY DEFICITS

The Trap

The first equity trap, seeing only deficits, draws from Valencia's (1997) work on deficit thinking. According to Valencia, the deficit-thinking model is

> an endogenous theory—a theory that posits that the student who fails in school does so principally because of internal deficits or deficiencies. Such deficiencies manifest, it is alleged, in limited intellectual abilities, linguistic shortcomings, lack of motivation to learn, and immoral behavior. (p. 2)

Thus, if a teacher or administrator has a deficit view, she or he may see students as being genetically inferior—"they're just not very smart"—or students and students' families are just not valuing education—"they just don't care about education"—or students as unmotivated and incapable of good behavior—"they just don't care about learning and can't behave well enough to learn."

The Skill: Developing an Asset View

There are, however, many teachers and administrators who have an asset view of their students and their families (as we mentioned in Chapter 8). These individuals see all their students as intellectually capable. They see their students and students' families as caring about and valuing education (Lopez, 2001). And they see the potential for all students to be motivated and engaged learners.

The Strategy

How, then, does one turn a deficit view into an asset view? This requires a reframing of thinking about students and their families. In this reframing, one recognizes that students and their families have funds of knowledge (for a complete discussion of this concept, see Moll, Amanti, Neff, & Gonzalez, 1992). These funds of knowledge are the strategies, abilities, practices, and ideas that children bring to school from their homes and communities (Gonzalez et al., 1993). When one learns to recognize and value these funds of knowledge as valuable qualities and skills, deficit thinking can be transformed into asset thinking. However, for school faculty and staff to acknowledge and value the funds of knowledge students bring with them to school, they must get to know their students and their students' families. Three tactics we and others have used to accomplish this are neighborhood walks, oral histories, and three-way conferencing (for more information regarding three-way conferencing, see Lam & Peake, 1997; Ricci, 2000). Here we provide a little more detail on one of these tactics—neighborhood walks. (For a complete discussion of all these strategies and tactics we have used to develop equity skills, see McKenzie & Scheurich, 2004.) Neighborhood walks have proven successful in getting school staffs to know their students and their students' families and communities at a deeper level. We have found that going door-to-door to every student's home to welcome students and their families to a new school year and also to invite them to partner with the school in the education process establishes positive rapport between the school and the home and community. Moreover, this is the start of turning a deficit view into an asset view. From our experiences, once school staffs get to know students and their families through positive exchanges, it is much easier for them to see the assets or funds of knowledge students and their families possess. Of course, it's not so simple.

Whereas neighborhood walks can initiate positive experiences, they need to be followed up with positive phone calls or notes home, personal invitations to school events, collaboration regarding school goals and individual student's goals, timely communication that is clear and in the students' home language, and so on. In other words, there needs to be multiple and genuine efforts to partner with families and communities in the education of their children.

EQUITY TRAP 2: ERASING RACE AND CULTURE

The Trap

The next equity trap is racial erasure. This concept comes from the work of bell hooks (1992). She defined racial erasure, which is often referred to as colorblindness, as "the sentimental idea . . . that racism would cease to exist if everyone would just forget about race and just see each other as human beings who are the same" (p. 12). One has to ask why individuals would want to see each other as the same when it is our differences that add texture and make life more interesting. This question aside, though, the idea that we can forget about race and just see each other as human beings seems to say that race is a bad thing, that one would have to overlook or get beyond someone's race to see them as human beings—to see them as "the same" not "the other."

The Skill: Seeing and Respecting Race and Culture

To prevent getting trapped into erasing race, in other words colorblindness, or to get out of this trap, one has to see and respect race. In other words, instead of trying to avoid seeing someone's difference, we should work toward *seeing* someone's difference and respecting that difference. This requires learning about ourselves and learning about our conscious and unconscious beliefs. We may have to ask ourselves, "Why do I try to erase someone's race? What is it about seeing some-one's skin color that makes me feel uncomfortable? Do I mentally try to avoid seeing the skin color of everyone or just people unlike myself? If I'm white, do I try to avoid seeing another white person's skin color, or do I not even think of white as a skin color, as race?"

The Strategy

One strategy we have used to help ourselves and others to become more racially and culturally aware and respectful is through learning groups. These are usually focused around a book, but they do not have to be. We and others have also used film; print sources, including journal articles, newspaper stories, and editorials; commercials from visual media; and art in varying forms. Some of our front-running colleagues are using the virtual world to create spaces for learning groups

(Brunner, Hitchon, & Brown, 2002; Lee & Hoadley, 2006). A caution, though: whichever format one uses for learning groups, the establishment, organization, and process of these groups need to be thoughtful. We suggest (as we have in earlier chapters) taking a look at Singleton and Linton's (2006) book, *Courageous Conversations About Race: A Field Guide for Achieving Equity in Schools*, for an example of a way these learning groups can be successfully structured.

EQUITY TRAP 3: RATIONALIZING BAD BEHAVIOR AND UNSUCCESSFUL PRACTICES

The Trap

This trap addresses two issues—treating students badly and maintaining practices that are unsuccessful and limit student learning. An example of the first issue would be the teacher or administrator who contends students must be dealt with harshly and punitively because it is the only behavior students understand or it is the only way to control students. An example of the second issue would be the teacher who will not incorporate classroom practices that allow students to work in collaborative groups (like science labs) or to get out of their seats and move around the room or to use manipulatives or to engage in any practices that require the teacher to relinquish strict teacher control. The notion here is that the only instructional arrangements that can work for some students are ones in which there are high levels of teacher control. In other words, the rationalization for not incorporating learning activities that would engage students is that the students just can't handle it. In both of these examples, the adults can maintain their current thinking and practices because they excuse their behavior or practices and frame the problem as residing outside themselves. In other words, the problem is not the way these adults think about or treat students; the problem is seen as the students. Therefore, this rationalizing of behavior and practices, this making of excuses, prevents reflection and the changing of beliefs and practices.

The Skill: Reflecting on Self

Self-reflection is critical for changing beliefs and practices (Vacc & Bright, 1999). When an individual shifts from externalizing and blaming others to internalizing and reflecting on one's own behavior, a space is created that can allow one to change beliefs and behaviors.

Self-reflection, however, is not something that occurs and then "one gets it." Self-reflection requires a nearly constant attention to thoughts and how these thoughts are manifested in behaviors and practices.

The Strategy

One cannot force someone else into self-reflection. Ultimately, it is a personal choice. Therefore, here we will discuss briefly some strategies we personally use to aid in our own self-reflection. The first is journaling. Daily journaling allows us to see what we think. It is writing our way to understanding. A second strategy is having a critical friend. Indeed, the three authors of this book often serve as critical friends to each other. A critical friend (Costa, 1993) is one that asks that tough question, which, to be answered, requires self-reflection. A third strategy to promote self-reflection is videotaping. Videotaping our teaching or speaking to a group and then watching the tape allows us to see and hear our beliefs and behaviors enacted. This is a powerful, albeit sometimes painful strategy.

EQUITY TRAP 4: NORMING THE NEGATIVE

The Trap

This final trap addresses the normalizing (in a negative way) of beliefs, behaviors, and practices. This means exerting group pressure on people within a school so that negativity becomes the *normal* situation for virtually all aspects of schooling. This is literally the opposite of having a positive school climate. This is the trap that takes all the others to scale. In other words, this is a collective trap that can ensnarl an entire school community. In this trap, there is a group within the school community that can prevent others from freeing themselves from the equity traps and developing equity skills. This is usually done in unconscious ways. For example, if a group of teachers are talking negatively about a particular student or that student's family and one of the teachers offers a counter view, the others in the group will *norm* the teacher into either tacitly accepting the negative view or just keeping silent and not pushing the positives.

This is done when one teacher says something and another agrees and then another, and when a counter opinion is offered, the group tells the individual who offered the counter opinion that the she or he "just doesn't know how it really is around here" or "it's always been this way and it's not going to change" or "you'll learn how things are here." Not only is this norming done in regard to opinions about students and their families, it is done in response to new teaching initiatives and efforts to involve the community, just about anything that would disrupt the status quo.

The Skill: Creating Transparency

It is difficult for in an individual, especially a new or inexperienced one, to resist the norming of a group. Again, though, keep in mind those who are most instrumental in the norming process are usually unaware of their participation in this process. So the skill to prevent or release an individual or whole school from this equity trap is to create transparency. Creating transparency means creating a school that is so thoroughly collaborative that all beliefs, behaviors, and practices are out in the open, are visible. Once made visible, deficit beliefs, inappropriate behaviors, and unsuccessful practices can be understood, addressed, and transformed.

The Strategy

The most successful strategy we have used to bring about transparency is through the teaching and learning tours described in Chapter 10. Not only do these tours provide in-situ professional development to assist teaching in developing as reflective practitioners, the tours serve as opportunities for teachers to sit in small groups and debrief. Our experience has been that during these debriefing sessions or as a result of these sessions, teachers become aware of or *see* their beliefs and how these beliefs form their behavior and practices. Just the other day in one of these sessions, we were discussing which students get left out of instruction or placed out of instruction. There was a great deal of talk about African American males being left out or moved out. The discussion was around trying to understand behaviors that seemed unruly to some of the teachers. However, one of us asked about the compliant student, in this case a Latina who was always quiet and respectful. This was an eye-opener. One teaching assistant, herself Latina, said, "Oh my gosh, I never thought about this. There is a student in our class right now who I assumed was learning, but maybe she's not. I'm going to check on her today and see."

Therefore, it was through this discussion that teacher assumptions about student learning behaviors became visible.

CHAPTER CONCLUSION

This chapter describes the traps that prevent educators from being successful with all students and the equity skills that prevent individuals and groups from falling into these traps or setting themselves free from the traps. Moreover, strategies to develop these equity skills are offered. This chapter concludes the discussion of equity audits and of strategies for addressing issues revealed by the audits. In the next chapter, Chapter 12, we provide concluding comments and reflections for the entire book.

DISCUSSION QUESTIONS AND ACTIVITIES

1. Do you see any of the equity traps described in this chapter as being present on your campus or in your district? Which one (if any) is the largest? Are any of the skills and strategies outlined here for addressing these traps currently in place in your school or district?

2. If your school is not currently doing neighborhood walks routinely, what could you do to get such an activity started? What steps would you need to take to make a plan for this type activity?

12 Conclusion

When it is obvious that the goals cannot be reached, don't adjust the goals, adjust the action steps.

—Confucius

In the previous eleven chapters of this book, we have laid out what we hope is a coherent set of actions that campus and district leaders can first use to assess their campuses and then to plan change for their schools to become more equitable and just places. The first step in this series of actions is, of course, the equity audit itself. We began our book by giving the history and background of the equity-audit concept and also making the case for the need for systemic equity. Next, we explained in detail the three main components of our version of equity audits: teacher quality equity, programmatic equity, and achievement equity.

Conducting the equity audit, however, though a critically important first step, is *only* the first step needed for campuses and districts to change. Once the data assembled for the equity audit has been analyzed and areas in need of improvement have been identified, school and district leaders and their staffs must work together to plan, implement, and evaluate their action steps. To assist educators in this work, in the third part of this book, we provided four chapters on strategies. These broad strategy areas include becoming an equity-oriented change agent as a leader, developing equity consciousness among teachers, promoting high-quality teaching skills, and avoiding equity traps.

It is our sincere hope that within these pages readers find concrete, immediately useful ideas that can be put in place in their schools and districts so that positive change can begin to change the beliefs, structures, and practices that reproduce inequity on a daily basis. We also hope that this book has provided the next level of depth and detail beyond our work in *Leadership for Equity and Excellence* that so many of our students and practitioners with whom we work have asked us for.

What occurs after you put down this book, however, is now up to you. What we've described and suggested in the book is really only the bare beginning of what is possible if you make a commitment to conduct an equity audit of your school or district and also commit to take seriously the implications for change that result from the findings. We have heard many amazing stories from practitioners who were inspired by our earlier, shorter version of equity audits to take bold steps in their local settings and to custom design their own approaches to both the audit and the action plan that followed. The North East ISD story that appears in Chapter 8 is just one example of this type of expansion on the idea of an equity audit made by practitioners with whom we have worked.

In the past, we've used the equity audit with school board members, practicing administrators, teachers, parents, and administrative students in our classes. Though there have been many tense conversations and uncomfortable moments in doing this work, *all* of these groups have, in the end, viewed the idea of an equity audit as a useful and valuable thing to do. So what will you do with it?

Whatever the answer to that question is, we wish you much success. As we noted at the end of our *Leadership for Equity and Excellence* book, we are all in the work of advancing equity in our schools together. We see it as both a civic and a spiritual responsibility to engage in such work. It is literally civil rights work for us all to be challenging educational inequity on a daily basis and working to change it.

Those of us who choose this civil rights work join a long line of amazing individuals who have come before us who worked and sacrificed to bring our society and our schools along as far as they have come today. This is noble and important work, and we wish each of you who is engaged in it much success.

References

Anderson, G. L. (2001). Promoting educational equity in a period of growing social inequity: The silent contradictions of the Texas reform discourse. *Education and Urban Society, 33*(3), 321–332.

Artiles, A. J. (1998). The dilemma of difference: Enriching the disproportionality discourse with theory and context. *Journal of Special Education, 32*(1), 32–36.

Ballou, D., Sanders, W., & Wright, P. (2004). Controlling for student background in value-added assessment of teachers. *Journal of Educational and Behavioral Statistics, 29*(1), 37–65.

Bandura, A., & Walters, R. H. (1963). *Social learning and personality development*. New York: Holt, Rinehart, and Winston.

Bell, L. I. (2003). Strategies that close the gap. *Educational Leadership, 60*(4), 32–34.

Berliner, D. C. (2001). Learning about and learning from expert teachers. *International Journal of Educational Research, 35*(5), 463–482.

Black, W. R., & Valenzuela, A. (2003). Educational accountability for English language learners in Texas: A retreat from equity. In L. Skrla & J. J. Scheurich (Eds.), *Educational equity and accountability: Policies, paradigms, and politics* (pp. 215–234). New York: RoutledgeFalmer.

Bock, R. D., & Wolfe, R. (1996). *A review and analysis of the Tennessee Value-Added Assessment System. Part I: Audit and review of the Tennessee Value-Added Assessment System (TVAAS): Final report*. Nashville, TN: Comptroller of the Treasury.

Boudett, K. P., Murnane, R. J., City, E., & Moody, L. (2005). Teaching educators how to use student assessment data to improve instruction. *Phi Delta Kappan, 86*(9), 700–706.

Bowman, D. H. (2003). Report finds suspension disparities in KY. *Education Week, 22*(25), 6.

Brunner, C. C., Hitchon, N. G., & Brown, R. (2002). Advancing social justice as a part of educational leadership development: The potential of imaging technologies. *On the Horizon, 10*(3), 12–15.

Cartledge, G., Tillman, L. C., & Talbert-Johnson, C. T. (2001). Professional ethics within the context of student discipline and diversity. *Teacher Education and Special Education, 24*(1), 25–37.

Chellman, C., Weinstein, M., Stiefel, L., & Schwartz, A. (2005). *Why do some schools succeed at closing the racial test score gap?* Paper presented at the annual meeting of the American Educational Research Association, Montreal, Quebec.

Cohen, D. K., & Hill, H. (2000). Instructional policy and classroom performance: The mathematics reform in California. *Teachers College Record, 102*(2): 294–343.

Cohen, D. K., & Hill, H. C. (2001). *Learning policy: When state education reform works*. New Haven, CT: Yale University Press.

College Board. (2001). *Access to excellence: A report of the commission on the future of the Advanced Placement Program.* New York: Author.

Costa, A. L. (1993). Through the lens of a critical friend. *Educational Leadership, 51*(2), 49–51.

Dantley, M. (2003). Critical spirituality: Enhancing transformative leadership through critical theory and African American prophetic spirituality. *International Journal of Leadership in Education, 6*(1), 3–17.

Darling-Hammond, L. (1999). *Teacher quality and student achievement: A review of state policy evidence*. Seattle: Center for the Study of Teaching and Learning.

Darling-Hammond, L. (2000). Teacher quality and student achievement: A review of state policy evidence. *Educational Policy Analysis Archives, 8*(1), Retrieved May 5, 2008, from http://www.epaa.asu.edu/

Darling-Hammond, L. (2001). The challenge of staffing our schools. *Educational Leadership, 58*(8), 12–17.

Denbo, S., Grant, C., & Jackson, S. (1994). *Educate America: A call for equity in school reform*. Chevy Chase, MD: National Coalition of Educational Equity Advocates.

Doran, H. C., & Fleischman, S. (2005). Challenges of value-added assessment. *Educational Leadership, 63*(3), 85–87.

Edmonds, R. R. (1979). Effective schools for the urban poor. *Educational Leadership, 37*(1), 15, 18, 20–24.

Education Trust. (2006). *Yes we can: Telling truths and dispelling myths about race and education in America.* Washington, DC: Author.

Elmore, R. F. (2002). Testing trap. *Harvard Magazine, 105*(1), 35.

English, F. W. (1988). *Curriculum auditing.* Lancaster, PA: Technomic.

Epp, J. R., & Watkinson, A. M. (1997). *Systemic violence in education: Promise broken*. Albany: State University of New York Press.

Ferguson, R. F. (1998). Teachers' perceptions and expectations and the Black-White test score gap. In C. Jencks & M. Phillips (Eds.), *The*

Black-White test score gap (pp. 318–375). Washington, DC: Brookings Institution Press.

Festinger, L. (1957). *A theory of cognitive dissonance*. Evanston, IL: Row Peterson.

Ford, D. Y., & Harmon, D. A. (2001). Equity and excellence: Providing access to gifted education for culturally diverse students. *Journal of Secondary Gifted Education, 11*(3), 141–148.

Fuller, E., & Berry, B. (2006). *Texas teacher quality data: Prospects and problems*. Hillsborough, NC: Center for Teaching Quality.

Gates, G. S., & Lichtenberg, K. (2005). Accountability data and decision making in Texas bilingual education programs. *Journal of Latinos in Education, 4*(4), 271–282.

Gay, G. (2000). *Culturally responsive teaching: Theory, research, and practice*. New York: Teachers College Press.

Goddard, R. D., Hoy, W. K., & Woolfolk, A. (2000). Collective teacher efficacy: Its meaning, measure, and effect on student achievement. *American Educational Research Journal, 37*(2), 479–507.

Gonzalez, M. L., & Huerta-Macias, A. (1997). Mi casa es su casa. *Educational Leadership, 55*(2), 52–55.

Gonzalez, N., Moll, L. C., Floyd-Tenery, M., Rivera, A., Gonzales, R., et al. (1993). *Teacher research on funds of knowledge: Learning from households*. Tucson, AZ: National Center for Research on Cultural Diversity and Second Language Learning.

Gregory, G. H. (2003). *Differentiated instructional strategies in practice*. Thousand Oaks, CA: Sage.

Gregory, J. F. (1995). The crime of punishment: Racial and gender disparities in the use of corporal punishment in U.S. schools. *Journal of Negro Education, 64*(4), 454–463.

Haney, W. (2001). Response to Skrla et al. The illusion of educational equity in Texas: A commentary on "accountability for equity." *International Journal of Leadership in Education, 4*(3), 2.

Haycock, K. (2001). Closing the achievement gap. *Educational Leadership, 58*(6).

Heck, R. H. (2007). Examining the relationship between teacher quality as an organizational property of schools and students' achievement and growth rates. *Educational Administration Quarterly, 43*(4), 399–432.

Hewson, P. W., Kahle, J. B., Scantlebury, K., & Davies, D. (2001). Equitable science education in urban middle schools: Do reform efforts make a difference? *Journal of Research in Science Teaching, 38*(10), 1130–1144.

Hill, H. C., Rowan, B., & Ball, D. L. (2005). Effects of teachers' mathematical knowledge for teaching on student achievement. *American Educational Research Journal, 42*(2), 371–406.

hooks, b. (1992). *Black looks: Race and representation*. Cambridge, MA: South End.

Hunter, M. (1994). *Mastery teaching*. Thousand Oaks, CA: Corwin.

Ingersoll, R. M. (1999). The problem of underqualified teachers in American secondary schools. *Educational Researcher, 28*(2), 26–37.

Institute for School-University Partnerships. (2001). *Research finds that 25 percent of newly-hired teachers for 2000–2001 not fully certified*. Bryan, TX: Author.

Kahle, J. (1998). *Researching equity in systemic reform: How do we assess progress and problems?* Madison, WI: National Institute for Science Teaching (ED 472 341).

Klein, S. (2001). Response to Skrla et al.: Is there a connection between educational equity and accountability? *International Journal of Leadership in Education, 4*(3), 261–266.

Ladson-Billings, G. (1995). But that's just good teaching! The case for culturally relevant pedagogy. *Theory Into Practice, 34*(3), 159–165.

Ladson-Billings, G. (1997). Toward a theory of culturally relevant pedagogy. *American Education Research Journal, 32*(3), 465–491.

Lam, Y., & Peake, R. (1997). Triad conference: Is it a more effective way of involving parents and students? *McGill Journal of Education, 32*(3), 249–262.

Lankford, H., Loeb, S., & Wyckoff, J. (2002). Teacher sorting and the plight of urban schools: A descriptive analysis. *Educational Evaluation and Policy Analysis, 24*(1), 37–62.

Lee, J. J., & Hoadley, C. M. (2006). "Ugly in a world where you can choose to be beautiful": Teaching and learning about diversity via virtual worlds. In S. Barab, D. Hickey, & K. Hay (Eds.), *Proceedings of the Seventh International Conference of the Learning Sciences* (pp. 383–389).

Lipsky, M. (1980). *Street-level bureaucracy: Dilemmas of the individual in public services*. New York: Russell Sage Foundation.

Lopez, G. R. (2001). Redefining parental involvement: Lessons from high-performing migrant-impacted schools. *American Educational Research Journal, 38*(2), 253–288.

Losen, D., & Orfield, G. (2002). *Racial inequity in special education*. Cambridge, MA: Harvard Education Publishing Group.

Love, N., Stiles, K. E., Mundry, S., & DiRanna, K. (2008). *The data coach's guide*. Acton, MA: Research for Better Teaching.

Lyman, L. L., & Villani, C. J. (2004). *Best leadership practices for high-poverty schools*. New York: Scarecrow.

MacMillan, D. L., & Reschy, D. J. (1998). Overrepresentation of minority students: The case for greater specificity or reconsideration of the variables examined. *Journal of Special Education, 32*(1), 15–24.

Marzano, R. J. (2003). *What works in schools*. Alexandria, VA: ASCD.

McCaffrey, D. F., Lockwood, J. R., Koretz, D. M., & Hamilton, L. S. (2003). *Evaluating value-added models for teacher accountability, MG-158-EDU.* Santa Monica, CA: RAND.

McCaffrey, D. F., Lockwood, J., Koretz. D. M., Louis, T. A., & Hamilton, L. (2004). Models for value-added modeling of teacher effects. *Journal of Educational and Behavioral Statistics, 29*(1), 67–101.

McDermott, R. P. (1997). Achieving school failure, 1972–1997. In G. Spindler, *Education and cultural process.* Prospect Heights, IL: Waveland Press.

McKenzie, K. B. (2001). *White teachers' perceptions about their students of color and themselves as white educators.* Dissertation, The University of Texas at Austin.

McKenzie, K. B. (2003). The unintended consequences of the Texas accountability system. In L. Skrla & J. J. Scheurich (Eds.), *Educational equity and accountability: Policies, paradigms, and politics* (pp. 235–250). New York: RoutledgeFalmer.

McKenzie, K. B., & Lozano, R. (2008). Teachers' zone of self-efficacy: Which students get included, which students get excluded, and more importantly, why? *The National Journal of Urban Education, 1*(4), 372–384.

McKenzie, K. B., & Scheurich, J. J. (2004). Equity traps: A useful construct for preparing principals to lead schools that are successful with racially diverse students. *Educational Administration Quarterly, 40*(5), 601–632.

McKenzie, K. B., Skrla, L., & Scheurich, J. (2006). Preparing instructional leaders for social justice. *Journal of School Leadership, 16*(2), 158–170.

Mezirow, J. (2000). *Learning as transformation.* San Francisco: Jossey-Bass.

Mitchell, J. K., & Poston, W. K. (1992). The equity audit in school reform: Three case studies of educational disparity and incongruity. *International Journal of Educational Reform, 1*(3), 242–247.

Moll, L. C. (1992). Bilingual classroom studies and community analysis: Some recent trends. *Educational Researcher, 20*(2), 20–24.

Moll, L. C., Amanti, C., & Gonzalez, N. (2005). *Funds of knowledge: Theorizing practices in households and classrooms.* Mahwah, NJ: Lawrence Erlbaum.

Moll, L. C., Amanti, C., Neff, D., & Gonzalez, N. (1992). Funds of knowledge for teaching: Using a qualitative approach to connect homes and classrooms. *Theory Into Practice, 31*(2), 132–141.

New Zealand Department of Labor. (2006). *Pay and employment equity unit.* Retrieved May 5, 2008, from http://www.dol.govt.nz/services/PayAnd Employment Equity/resources/assessment-tools.asp

No Child Left Behind Act of 2001, Pub. L. No. 107–100. Retrieved May 5, 2008, from http://www.ed.gov/legislation/ESEA02/

Oakes, J. (1986). *Keeping track: How schools structure inequality*. New Haven, CT: Yale University Press.

O'Day, J. A. (2002). Complexity, accountability, and school improvement. *Harvard Educational Review, 72*(3), 293–329.

Parker, L. (2001). Statewide assessment triggers urban school reform: But how high the stakes for urban minorities? *Education and Urban Society, 33*(3), 313–320.

Pollock, M. (2001). How the questions we ask most about race in education is the very question we most suppress. *Educational Researcher, 30*(9), 2–12.

Poston, W. K. (1992). The equity audit in school reform: Building a theory for educational research. *International Journal of Educational Reform, 1*(3), 235–241.

Prince, C. D. (2002). *The challenge of attracting good teachers and principals to struggling schools*. Arlington, VA: American Association of School Administrators.

Raudenbush, S. W. (2004). What are value added models estimating and what does that imply for statistical practice? *Journal of Educational and Behavioral Statistics, 29*(1), 121–129.

Resnick, L. B., & Hall, M. W. (2001). *The principles of learning: Study tools for educators* [CD-ROM, version 2.0]. Pittsburgh: University of Pittsburgh, Learning Research and Development Center, Institute for Learning (www.instituteforlearning.org).

Ricci, B. (2000). How about parent-teacher-student conferences? *Principal, 79*(5), 53–54.

Rice, J. K. (2003). *Teacher quality: Understanding the effectiveness of teacher attributes*. Washington, DC: Economic Policy Institute.

Rivkin, S., Hanushek, E., & Kain, J. (2001). Teachers, schools, and academic achievement. A working paper for the *National Bureau of Economics Research*.

Rockoff, J. E. (2004). The impact of individual teachers on student achievement: Evidence from panel data. *American Economic Review, 94*(2), 247–252.

Rorrer, A. K., & Skrla, L. (2005). Leaders as policy mediators. *Theory Into Practice, 44* (1), 53–62.

Rorrer, A. K., Skrla, L., & Scheurich, J. J. (2008). Districts as institutional actors in educational reform. *Educational Administration Quarterly, 44*(3), 307–357.

Rowan, B., Correnti, R., & Miller, R. J. (2002). What large-scale survey research tells us about teacher effects on student achievement: Insights from the Prospects Study of Elementary Schools. *Teachers College Record, 104*, 1525–1567.

Sanders, W. L., & Rivers, J. C. (1996). *Cumulative and residual effects of teachers on future student academic achievement*. Knoxville, TN:

University of Tennessee Value-Added Research and Assessment Center.

Saphier, J., Haley-Speca, M. A., & Gower, R. (2008). *The skillful teacher.* Acton, MA: Research for Better Teaching.

Scheurich, J. J., & Skrla, L. (2003). *Leadership for equity and excellence: Creating high-achievement classrooms, schools, and districts.* Thousand Oaks, CA: Corwin.

Scheurich, J. J., Skrla, L., & Johnson, J. F. (2000). Thinking carefully about equity and accountability. *Phi Delta Kappan, 82*(4), 293–299.

Schoenfeld, A. H. (2002). Making mathematics work for all children: Issues of standards, testing, and equity. *Educational Researcher, 3*(1), 13–25.

Sclafani, S. (2001). Using an aligned system to make real progress for Texas students. *Education and Urban Society, 33*(3), 305–312.

Scott, B. (2001, March). Coming of age. *IDRA Newsletter* [On-line]. Retrieved May 7, 2008, from http://www.idra.org/IDRA_Newsletter/March_2001_Self_Renewing_Schools_Access_Equity_and_Excellence/Coming_of_Age/

Singleton, G. E., & Linton, C. (2006). *Courageous conversations about race: A field guide for achieving equity in schools.* Thousand Oaks, CA: Sage.

Sizer, T. (1997). *Horace's hope: What works for the American high school.* New York: Mariner Books.

Skiba, R., & Noam, G. (Eds.). (2001). *Zero tolerance: Can suspension and expulsion keep schools safe.* San Francisco: Jossey-Bass.

Skrla, L. (2001). Accountability, equity, and complexity. *Educational Researcher, 30*(4), 15–21.

Skrla, L., & Scheurich, J. J. (2001). Displacing deficit thinking in school district leadership. *Education and Urban Society, 33*(3), 235–259.

Skrla, L., Scheurich, J. J., & Johnson, J. F. (2000). *Equity-driven, achievement focused school districts: A report on systemic school success in four Texas school districts serving diverse student populations.* Austin, TX: The Charles A. Dana Center. Retrieved May 5, 2008, from http://utdirect.utexas.edu/txshop/item_details.WBX?cart_id=0MHDANACT&dept_prefix=MH&item_id=76&cat_seq_chosen=04&subcategory_seq_chosen=000&r_cust_service_url=http://www.utdanacenter.org/customerservice/index.html

Skrla, L., Scheurich, J. J., & Johnson, J. F. (2001). Toward a new consensus on high academic achievement for all children. *Education and Urban Society, 33*(3), 227–234.

Skrla, L., Scheurich, J. J., Johnson, J. F., & Koschoreck, J. W. (2001a). Accountability for equity: Can state policy leverage social justice? *International Journal of Leadership in Education, 4*(3), 237–260.

Skrla, L., Scheurich, J. J., Johnson, J. F., & Koschoreck, J. W. (2001b). Complex and contested constructions of accountability and educational equity. *International Journal of Leadership in Education, 4*(3), 277–283.

Sleeter, C. E. (1996). *Multicultural education as social activism.* Albany, NY: State University of New York Press.

Smith, M., & O'Day, J. (1990). Systemic school reform. In S. Fuhrman & B. Malen (Eds.), *The politics of curriculum and testing* (pp. 233–267). New York: Routledge.

Smith, T. M., Desimone, L. M., & Ueno, K. (2005). "Highly qualified" to do what? The relationship between NCLB teacher quality mandates and the use of reform-oriented instruction in middle school mathematics. *Educational Evaluation and Policy Analysis, 29*(3), 169–199.

Steffy, B. (1993). *The Kentucky education reform.* Lanham, MD: Scarecrow Press.

Taylor, K., Marienau, C., & Fiddler, M. (2000). *Developing adult learners.* San Francisco: Jossey-Bass.

Tennessee Department of Education. (2002). *Tennessee value-added assessment system.* Retrieved May 5, 2008, from https://tvaas.sas.com/evaas/public_welcome.jsp

Texas Center for Educational Research. (2000). *Strengthened assessment and accountability.* Austin, TX: Author.

Tomlinson, C. A. (1999). Mapping a route toward differentiated instruction. *Educational Leadership, 57*(1), 12–16.

Tomlinson, C. A., Brighton, C., Hertberg, H., Callahan, C. M., Moon, T. R., Brimijoin, K., et al. (2003). Differentiating instruction in response to student readiness, interest, and learning profile in academically diverse classrooms: A review of literature. *Journal for the Education of the Gifted, 27*(2,3), 119–145.

Townsend, B. L. (2002). "Testing while Black": Standards-based school reform and African American learners. *Remedial and Special Education, 23*(4), 222–231.

Trueba, H. (2001). Polar positions on the Texas Assessment of Academic Skills (TAAS): Pragmatism and the politics of neglect. *Education and Urban Society, 33*(3), 333–344.

U.S. Department of Education Office of Civil Rights. (1999). *Impact of civil rights laws.* Washington, DC: Author.

Vacc, N. N., & Bright, G. W. (1999). Elementary preservice teachers' changing beliefs and instructional use of children's mathematical thinking. *Journal for Research in Mathematics Education, 30*(1), 89–110.

Valencia, R. R. (1997). *The evolution of deficit thinking: Educational thought and practice.* London: Falmer.

Valencia, R. R., Valenzuela, A., Sloan, K., & Foley, D. E. (2001). Let's treat the cause, not the symptoms: Equity and accountability in Texas revisited. *Phi Delta Kappan, 83*(4), 318–321.

Wehlage, G. G., & Rutter, R. A. (1986). Dropping out: How much do schools contribute to the problem? *Teachers College Record, 87*(3), 374–392.

Wheelock, A. (1993). *Crossing the tracks.* New York: John Muir Publications.

Williamson, P., Bondy, E., Langley, L., Mayne, D. (2005). Meeting the challenges of high-stakes testing while remaining child-centered: The representations of two urban teachers. *Childhood Education, 81*(4), 190–195.

Wisconsin Department of Public Instruction. (2008). *Pupil nondiscrimination glossary of terms.* Retrieved August 24, 2008, from http://165.189.80.100/sped/pndg-gloss.html

Wong, H. K., & Wong, R. T. (2004). *The first days of school.* Mountain View, CA: Harry K. Wong.

Yair, G. (2000). Not just about time: Instructional practices and productive time in school. *Educational Administration Quarterly, 36*(4), 485–512.

Index

Page references followed by *fig* indicate an illustrated figure, followed by *t* indicate a table.

CORWIN

A SAGE Company

The Corwin logo—a raven striding across an open book—represents the union of courage and learning. Corwin is committed to improving education for all learners by publishing books and other professional development resources for those serving the field of PreK–12 education. By providing practical, hands-on materials, Corwin continues to carry out the promise of its motto: **"Helping Educators Do Their Work Better."**

NSDC's purpose: Every educator engages in effective professional learning every day so every student achieves.

NATIONAL ASSOCIATION OF SECONDARY SCHOOL PRINCIPALS

Promoting Excellence in School Leadership

The National Association of Secondary School Principals—promoting excellence in school leadership since 1916—provides its members the professional resources to serve as visionary leaders. NASSP further promotes student leadership development through its sponsorship of the National Honor Society®, the National Junior Honor Society®, and the National Association of Student Councils®. For more information, visit www.principals.org.

Use the power of EQUITY AUDITS to help eliminate achievement gaps and educational bias!

If you've heard about equity audits but aren't really sure how to use them in your school, you are not alone. This resource, written by well-known experts in the areas of equity and achievement, expands school leaders' understanding of how to interpret data to make equity audits work. The authors provide practical, easy-to-implement strategies for using this school assessment approach to ensure a high-quality education for all students, regardless of socioeconomic class.

Grounded solidly in theory, this book demonstrates how audits can help not only in developing fair programs that provide all students with the opportunity to reach their potential, but also for hiring, training, and retaining good teachers. Readers will discover how to remedy inequalities in student achievement by using

- A set of "inequity indicators" for evaluating schools, generating essential data, and identifying problem areas
- The NCLB Act in a positive way to create equity
- Nine skill sets for improved equity-oriented teaching
- Charts, graphs, and support materials that can be customized for specific settings

Ideal for helping principals develop school-based equity audits with confidence, *Using Equity Audits to Create Equitable and Excellent Schools* can also be used by superintendents to increase equity awareness at the district level.

CORWIN
A SAGE Company

2455 Teller Road
Thousand Oaks, CA 91320
T: (800) 233-9936
F: (800) 417-2466
CorwinPress.com

ISBN 978-1-4129-3932-4

90000

9 781412 939324